Gooseberry Patch

HOMEMADE
Christmas

Gooseberry Patch

An imprint of Globe Pequot
246 Goose Lane
Guilford, CT 06437

www.gooseberrypatch.com

1•800•854•6673

Copyright 2021, Gooseberry Patch 978-1-62093-443-2

Photo Edition is a major revision of *Homemade Christmas.*

Do you have a tried & true recipe...

tip, craft or memory that you'd like to see featured in
a **Gooseberry Patch** cookbook? Visit our website at
www.gooseberrypatch.com and follow the
easy steps to submit your favorite family recipe.
Or send them to us at:

Gooseberry Patch
PO Box 812
Columbus, OH 43216-0812

Don't forget to include the number of servings your recipe makes,
plus your name, address, phone number and email address. If we
select your recipe, your name will appear right along with it...
and you'll receive a **FREE** copy of the book!

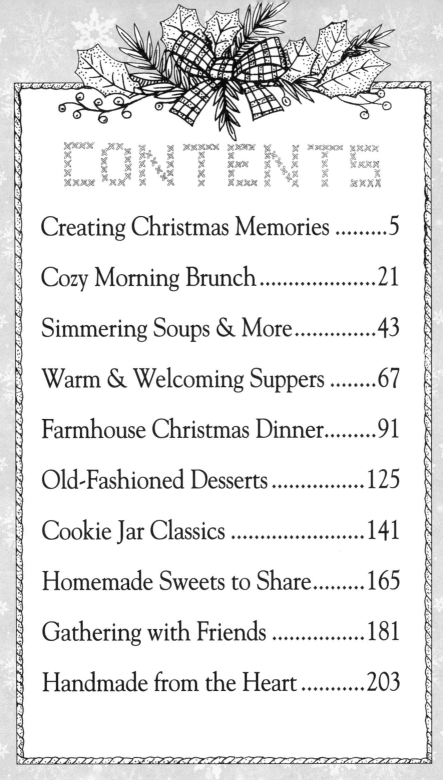

CONTENTS

Creating Christmas Memories 5

Cozy Morning Brunch 21

Simmering Soups & More..............43

Warm & Welcoming Suppers 67

Farmhouse Christmas Dinner.........91

Old-Fashioned Desserts 125

Cookie Jar Classics 141

Homemade Sweets to Share.........165

Gathering with Friends 181

Handmade from the Heart 203

Dedication

Dedicated to our friends who
love a homemade Christmas
best of all!

Appreciation

To those who shared cherished
recipes and memories, thanks!
May your Christmas be
merry & bright.

CREATING CHRISTMAS
Memories

Christmas Eve Chili Supper

Krystal Ruiz
Las Vegas, NV

Last Christmas we started a new family tradition. My husband is on active duty in the military, so we never know if we will be with family & friends at Christmas. All the people we know from the base may have moved on and no longer be stationed with us. So, this past Christmas Eve we invited all of my husband's co-workers and their families over for a chili cook-off and games. Because Christmas Day is usually filled with a lot of hustle & bustle cooking turkey and ham and preparing all the fixin's, we wanted to do something easy but delicious and filling. It turned out so well! I will never forget the smell of six different kinds of chili warming in the kitchen along with fresh rolls, bread and hot apple cider. I made Chicken Tomatillo Chili from my dad's own special recipe. People ended up enjoying three bowls of chili...or more!...and eating it all throughout the evening, during games and Wii challenges. It was a fantastic gathering, and a tradition that my family plans to continue for many years. Whether far or near, with new friends or old, it is nice to know there's something that will bring people all together to celebrate the season of Christ's birth!

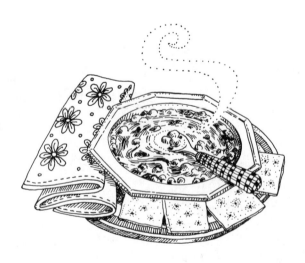

A Warm Christmas Glow

Randi Waldvogel
Wantagh, NY

A tradition we share as a family and look forward to every year is the lighting of our Advent candles. During the four weeks of Advent, we gather 'round the Christmas tree, light the candles and read a portion of scripture. Then we take turns choosing a Christmas carol. We sing with all the lights turned off except for the Advent candles and the Christmas tree lights. It is so beautiful! Now that our children are older, they take turns lighting the Advent candles as well as reading the scriptures. It is a delightful way to come together as a family, while keeping our hearts and minds focused on the true meaning of Christmas.

Family Ornament Swap

Michelle Dicus
Prairie Village, KS

Every Christmas Eve, my family holds an ornament exchange. Each person comes prepared with a gift-wrapped ornament. We gather in a circle and begin to read "'Twas the Night Before Christmas." Every time we read the word "the," we pass the ornament in our hands one person to the left. Every year, some jokester tries to sneak in extra "the's" to see if anybody catches them! After we've finished reading the story, everyone opens their ornament and oohs and ahhs. We definitely allow trading...there are no strict rules to the ornament exchange. My aunt started this activity many years ago and, although she is no longer with us, her memory lives on with this whimsical tradition!

Caroling, Caroling

Becky Woods
Ballwin, MO

I work at a local hospital where, for many years, a group of employees and their families would gather on Christmas Eve. First we attended a church service together, then a community dinner. The best part was last, when we would split up in small groups and sing Christmas carols door-to-door throughout the hospital. What a meaningful way to lead into our Christmas Day!

Twelve Days of Cheer

Anita Duvall
Clarksville, TN

I started a tradition several years ago with my grandmother. After my grandfather had passed away, she was very lonely, but kept her spirits high. She always loved all the holidays and most especially Christmas. I wrapped a gift for her for each of the twelve days before Christmas, ending on Christmas Day. She knew nothing of my surprise until the box arrived on her doorstep. She always looked forward to opening that gift each day, and would set it on her bedside table the night before. Grandmother loved this tradition for the rest of her life. Now I still carry on this tradition each year with my mother and daughter. I also choose someone different each year to receive the surprise. I have done this for friends, co-workers, and even some elderly people I have encountered in my job. I always hope to bring a little holiday cheer and the spirit of giving to someone else.

A New Home for Christmas

Lori Collins
Johnson City, TN

When I was eight, my mom and dad were building a new house just down the hill from where we lived. They worked on it every day, and my sister Melissa and I would join in with things we could do, too. My mom was determined that we were going to be moved in by Christmas that year...so, move we did. Only, when we moved in, the new house was not all done yet. We had to hang quilts and sheets over the door frames to keep the drafts out. But it was a beautiful Christmas lit by the tree. Mom even made these little clothespin ornaments with tiny candleholders that we lit all over the tree. What a wonderful Christmas...that was twenty years ago and it still stays in my memory...how magical and fun it was.

Firetruck Santa Claus

Dawn Tomeski
Bridgeville, DE

When I was a child, my fondest memories of Christmas took place on Christmas Eve day. While Mom was getting everything ready for the big night, my brothers and I would watch Christmas movies and listen for the siren of the firetruck. Our local fire department would drive all around with Santa on the back of the truck. We lived out in the country and Santa would stop at our home and visit with us, bringing each of us a box of hard candy and an orange. It really helped to make the day of anticipation a bit easier once Santa arrived. I still think of this whenever I hear a fire truck at Christmastime.

Twenty-Five Days of Memories
Darlene Strohmeyer
Rice Lake, WI

The year my daughter, Dawn Marie, was a student in England, she was not able to come home for the holidays, so I thought about how to make her holiday extra special. So I purchased twenty-five different, inexpensive Christmas cards and wrote a special family holiday memory in each one. I numbered the envelopes and put them in a special Christmas gift bag. Starting December 1st, she was able to open a card each day through Christmas. She loved being a part of our holiday and sharing our special holiday memories.

Dolly Christmas Pajamas
Michelle Campo
Methuen, MA

Every Christmas Eve when I was growing up, we'd go to my aunt & uncle's house. My mother would pack the new pajamas she had made for my sister, Melissa, and me, as well as the matching pajamas she made for our dolls. We'd stay out until late in the evening, putting our pajamas on at about 9 p.m., all excited to have the matching pajamas for our dolls. All the kids would gather around the Christmas tree for a photo...but my sister and I were the only ones who had pajamas that matched our dolls' pajamas! What great fun it was!

Helen's Thoughtful Gift

Debra Arch
Kewanee, IL

A few months before my ninth Christmas, our next-door neighbor, Helen, asked me if I would help her with her Christmas sewing. She said she was making a housecoat for her granddaughter, who was the same size as me, and she needed someone to model it so she could adjust the size and length of sleeves and hem. As I stood in the housecoat while Helen measured, I daydreamed about how beautiful the color and texture of the fabric was and how lucky the granddaughter would be when she opened up such a wonderful gift on Christmas. When she was done measuring, Helen thanked me for helping her and I returned home. Little did I know that Helen did not have a granddaughter my age...and on Christmas morning, under the tree was the beautiful housecoat, a gift from Helen to me! I have never forgotten how impressed I was with Helen's creativity and sewing skills. Her talents inspired me to learn to sew and give my own handmade gifts to others. Over the years, my skills grew, and I was pleased to be able to return the kindness to Helen by helping her with a couple of quilts she was making to give as gifts. Helen is gone now, but her generous gift of her time and talents in making me the housecoat as a young child will stay in my heart forever.

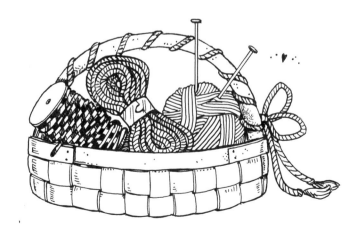

Smokey the Snow Bear

Carol Hickman
Kingsport, TN

When I was between the ages of two and seven years old,
my mom, dad and I lived in South Carolina. I looked forward every
Christmas to traveling to the mountains of Virginia to spend the
holidays with my grandparents. However, one Christmas when I
was about five years old, there came an unusually heavy snowfall
(for South Carolina, that is!) and we were unable to make the trip
to Virginia for Christmas. I was so disappointed because I dearly
loved spending time with my Mamaw Brickey. My dad, realizing
my disappointment and also wanting to take advantage of the deep
snow, took me outside and together we made a Smokey the Bear
snowman. I was thrilled with it, and how it looked just like Smokey!
So, instead of remembering that Christmas with disappointment,
I look back at it and remember how much fun it was to play in the
snow with Dad. I only wish we had thought to take a picture of
that "snow bear"...it was a masterpiece!

Twelve Books of Christmas

Charlene Rinehart
Washington, PA

As a family of readers, we love to share the gift of books with our children. Yet, books somehow don't always seem to get the special attention they deserve when piled under the tree with other goodies. So, my husband and I came up with the idea of celebrating "The Twelve Books of Christmas" with our children. Throughout the year we purchase books from various bookstores and catalogs, taking advantage of any bargains or sales. We stash them away for our special holiday tradition. After Christmas, our sons, Tim and Peter, are presented with large gift bags in which we have placed their twelve books of Christmas. Each night, for twelve nights, the boys are allowed to select one book from their bag. When the boys were small and selected picture books, we read the books the same night they were selected. As they got older and received chapter books, we savored each book by predicting what it would be about, reading a few pages together or looking at the illustrations, motivating the boys to read them on their own or begin a shared read-aloud with us. Our boys love this special tradition...and we sent the message that books are a delightful gift to be treasured!

Homemade Twig Stars

Amy Hunt
Traphill, NC

This past Christmas, I wanted to put a little old-fashioned touch on our holiday celebration with family, so my sister-in-law, Vicki, decided we should exchange homemade ornaments. My family made the twig Christmas tree and twig star ornaments from the **Gooseberry Patch Christmas Book #1.** We had a good time looking for the right-size twigs together to make our ornaments. Everyone loved them! It was nice to see everyone's creativity in their ornaments. We've decided to make this an annual family tradition and I will be looking through my many **Gooseberry Patch** Christmas books for more ideas.

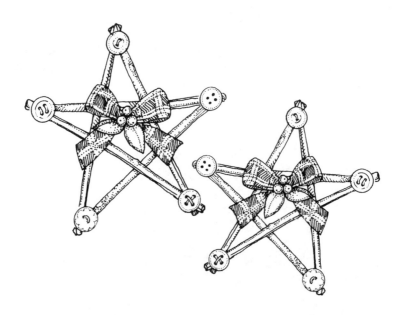

A Christmas Gift of Love

Pamela Elkin
Asheville, NC

On Christmas mornings when I was a young girl, our house was full of warmth and love with my siblings, parents, grandparents and great-grandparents. We savored a large Christmas breakfast, opened gifts together and then everyone came back later for our big Christmas dinner. This was our tradition every year. I guess I thought it was that way in everyone's home...until one special Christmas morning in the mid 1960s.

I was eight years old, my sister, Debbie, was eleven and my younger brother, Robby, was three. On that Christmas morning, after having breakfast and opening gifts, Mother and Daddy started gathering things together. They told us that we were going visiting. A man my daddy knew had called him that morning...they had no heat and no money. It was a very cold day. My parents suggested that we gather some gifts for the man's children. Debbie and I took some of the toys that we had gotten from Santa and went along with Daddy. I still remember going into that cold house. Daddy took in food and some oil for their heater, while my sister and I took in our gifts to the children. It was such a different Christmas morning in that cold house from what we had just had at home. Even though I was very young and this was many years ago, I still remember the little girl holding onto a fashion doll we'd given her and how happy she was.

That morning made a lasting impression in my heart. The older I have gotten, the more I have realized that even though we were not wealthy, my family was able to take the warmth and love from our own home and share it with a family who was so in need of it. That is what Christmas is all about, sharing the greatest gift...love. I am so glad that my parents taught me how to share love at a very young age. This is a lesson that I have tried to share with my two sons as well. Love is a priceless gift, yet it is so easy to give!

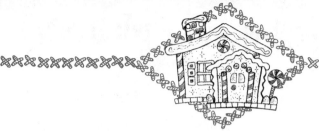

Happy Christmas Memories

Patty Schultz
Stevens Point, WI

When I was a child, our church always had a real Christmas tree.
We would all gather to decorate it and sing Christmas carols. What
a great time! Christmas Eve was the candlelight service, when you
got to light the next person's candle with your own little candle
while singing "Silent Night." Afterwards, we kids would all be
given brown paper bags filled with peanuts, an apple and some
peppermint nougat candy chews. It was so exciting! Then we would
head over to my dear Aunt Ann's house for more carols and some
of her famous meatballs. It was so much fun just to race home and
get tucked in bed so Santa could come. On Christmas morning, it
was rise & shine to sing "Happy Birthday" to Jesus. Such great
memories of growing up!

Now I've started some meaningful traditions with my own children.
We go to our Christmas Eve service and on Christmas morning we
read the Christmas story from the Bible. Then we open our gifts,
which are limited to three per person, because Baby Jesus received
three gifts. It's a great tradition and a way to follow His example.
I hope my children will cherish their Christmas memories as much
as I have mine!

Christmas at Granny's

Jeri Grant
Louisville, KY

My grandmother (the perfect granny) lived in a small town in the hills of eastern Kentucky. My Aunt Dorothy and Uncle Bill lived with her. Their home was always lovely, and at Christmas it was decorated for the holiday and especially welcoming. My parents and I lived over two hundred miles away and it was such a treat to spend Christmas at Granny's. The ornaments on Granny's tree were beautiful and, of course, the tree was always real. She would whip a mixture of soap flakes and water and spread it on the branches of the tree. After it hardened, it looked like a layer of sparkling snow had fallen on each branch. In a little girl's eyes, those were the most gorgeous Christmas trees ever to be seen. While her Christmas trees were beautiful, it is the feelings of security, safety and sheer happiness evoked by Christmas at Granny's that I remember most. My granny has been gone for thirty-seven years, but I still remember well her love for me and the Christmas memories she and my aunt and uncle created for me.

Mom's Christmas Gingerbread

Lisa Ashton
Aston, PA

This is a Christmas tradition that my mom has done for several years now, and we always look forward to it. Every Christmas, my mom loves to prepare some sort of display in gingerbread. Years ago, she would create her own paper templates for a gingerbread house or church. She'd cut them out of paper, then my father would re-cut them in cardboard, so they would be sturdier. The grandchildren would come a week or so before Christmas and decorate the house or church with all sorts of candy and icing. These past few years, my mom decided to do something different. She created a display of gingerbread people designed to look like each of her grandchildren. She molds each one of them by hand and gives them the physical appearance of one of the kids. When they are done, she uses icing to stand them up in a wintry display. It's such fun to go to her house to see them all in a group... the kids smile to see themselves as gingerbread people!

COZY MORNING
Brunch

Cherry Streusel Coffee Cake

Joyceann Dreibellis
Wooster, OH

This easy-to-assemble coffee cake recipe won "Best of Show" several years ago at our county fair and it's been requested at many social events. No wonder...it's irresistible!

18-1/2 oz. pkg. yellow cake
   mix, divided
1 env. active dry yeast
1 c. all-purpose flour
2 eggs, beaten

2/3 c. warm water
5 T. butter, melted
14-1/2 oz. can cherry pie filling
2 T. sugar
Garnish: chopped nuts

Combine 1-1/2 cups dry cake mix, yeast, flour, eggs and warm water; stir for 2 minutes. Spread in a greased 13"x9" baking pan. Blend melted butter and remaining cake mix; set aside. Spoon pie filling over batter in pan. Crumble butter mixture over pie filling. Sprinkle sugar over top. Bake at 375 degrees for 30 minutes. Let cool. Drizzle glaze over cooled cake; sprinkle nuts on top. Serves 15.

Glaze:

1 c. powdered sugar
1 T. corn syrup

1 to 2 T. water

Combine powdered sugar and corn syrup. Stir in enough water to form a glaze consistency.

If you're starting a weekend packed with Christmas activities, treat the family to a scrumptious homecooked breakfast first! After waffles or coffee cake, crispy bacon and eggs-your-way, everyone will be ready to take on sledding, shopping, decorating and more.

Mrs. Claus' Christmas Bread

Francie Stutzman
Dalton, Ohio

Packed with delicious fruit and nuts...share a loaf with a friend!

1 c. sugar	1/2 t. baking soda
2 T. butter, softened	1/2 t. salt
1 egg, beaten	3/4 c. orange juice
2 c. all-purpose flour	1 c. cranberries, chopped
1 t. baking powder	1/2 c. chopped pecans

Blend sugar, butter and egg together in a large bowl. Add remaining ingredients; mix well and pour into a greased 9"x5" loaf pan. Bake at 350 degrees for 45 to 50 minutes. Makes one loaf.

A loaf of homemade quick bread is always a welcome gift... it can even be made ahead one to two months and frozen. To make sure it stays oven-fresh, let the bread cool completely, then wrap well first in aluminum foil, then in festive holiday-print plastic wrap.

Christmas Morn Sausage Bake

Sheila Lowans
Bahama, NC

My mother used to fix this casserole for Christmas morning every year. Now I fix it for my own family, and I hope to pass it on to my girls too.

6 slices bread
1 lb. ground pork breakfast
  sausage, browned, drained
  and divided
1 c. shredded Swiss cheese

1 c. shredded Cheddar cheese
3 eggs, beaten
2 c. milk
salt to taste

Place 3 bread slices in the bottom of a greased 1-1/2 quart casserole dish. Spread half of sausage over bread; spread half of cheeses over sausage. Repeat layers. Beat eggs, milk and salt together; pour over top. Bake, uncovered, at 350 degrees for one hour. Serves 6 to 8.

...if it is going to be our kind of Christmas,
most of the presents will be homemade.

–Robert P. Tristram Coffin

Spinach & Mozzarella Quiche

Patricia Smith
Tehachapi, CA

One of my friends from church insists on having a piece of this quiche whenever I make it...it's quick, easy and delicious!

5-oz. pkg. baby spinach
2 T. water
9-inch deep-dish pie crust
1 c. shredded mozzarella
   cheese
3 eggs, beaten
1/2 c. sour cream
1/2 c. half-and-half
Optional: 3/4 c. ground pork
   sausage, browned and
   drained
nutmeg, salt and pepper
   to taste

In a saucepan over medium heat, steam spinach in water for 2 minutes. Drain well; press moisture out of spinach and sprinkle spinach over pie crust. Sprinkle cheese evenly over spinach. Whisk together remaining ingredients and pour over cheese. Bake at 325 degrees for 50 minutes. Let cool for 10 minutes before cutting. Makes 6 servings.

Nestle a sparkling punch bowl for brunch in the prettiest wreath. Wrap mini gift boxes in scraps of gift wrap and hot-glue then to a wreath form, then tuck in tiny, shiny ornament balls between the boxes.

Apple Pancake Syrup

Gail Shepard
Missoula, MT

*My older sister, Teena, often cooked for my siblings and me. She would
make this syrup to serve on our breakfast pancakes and waffles...
she could really make something from nothing!*

6-oz. can frozen sugar-free
   apple juice concentrate,
   thawed
3/4 c. water

1/2 t. lemon juice
1 T. cornstarch
1/4 t. cinnamon

Mix all ingredients in a saucepan. Cook over medium heat, stirring
frequently, until thickened and reduced by half, about 15 minutes.
Serves 4 to 6.

Winter Fried Apples

Cheri Emery
Quincy, IL

These buttery, tender apples are scrumptious on hotcakes.

1/4 c. butter
4 to 6 Jonathan apples, cored
   and sliced
1/2 t. cinnamon

2 T. sugar
2 T. brown sugar, packed
1/4 t. salt

Melt butter in a heavy cast-iron skillet over low heat. Add unpeeled
apple slices; sprinkle with remaining ingredients. Cook over medium
heat until apples are tender, 10 to 15 minutes. Serve warm. Makes
4 servings.

A chilly winter morning just seems to call for pancakes!
Make lots of 'em in a jiffy. Pour batter into an empty,
clean squeeze bottle, ready to squeeze out portions
right onto a hot griddle.

Baked Brown Sugar Oatmeal

Kim Travetti
Norristown, PA

*We enjoyed this oatmeal at the first bed & breakfast we ever
stayed at. Now it has become a staple for family breakfasts at
Christmas and Easter. It tastes like a warm oatmeal cookie!*

1/2 c. oil
2 eggs, beaten
1/2 c. brown sugar, packed
1/2 c. sugar
3 c. quick-cooking oats,
  uncooked

2 t. baking powder
1 t. salt
1 c. milk
Optional: raisins, brown sugar,
  milk

Whisk together oil, eggs and sugars; set aside. In a separate bowl,
combine oats, baking powder and salt; add to oil mixture. Add milk
and stir well. Pour into a greased 1-1/2 quart casserole dish. Bake,
uncovered, at 350 degrees for 45 minutes, or until top is golden.
Serve warm, either plain or garnished as desired. Serves 6.

Take the whole family to select and cut a Christmas tree...
an old tradition that's worth keeping. A hearty breakfast
of hot oatmeal will fortify everyone against the cold. Have
hot cocoa waiting in a slow cooker to chase away the chill
afterwards...with candy-cane stirrers just for fun!

Crispy Maple Bacon

Wendy Jacobs
Idaho Falls, ID

Oh my goodness, this bacon is so delicious! If my husband's brothers are coming over for our holiday brunch, I know I'll need to double the recipe...they can make a meal of it!

1 lb. sliced bacon
1/2 c. maple syrup

1 t. Dijon mustard

Line the bottom of a broiler pan with heavy-duty aluminum foil. Add broiler pan grill and spray with non-stick vegetable spray. Arrange bacon slices in a single layer. Combine syrup and mustard in a small bowl; drizzle half of mixture over bacon. Bake, uncovered, at 400 degrees for 12 to 15 minutes. Turn bacon over; baste with desired amount of remaining syrup mixture. Bake an additional 5 to 10 minutes, to desired crispness. Drain on paper towels; cool for several minutes before serving. Serves 6.

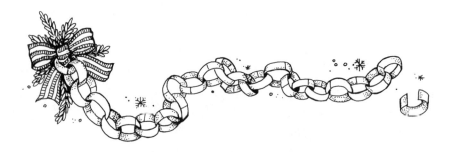

To little ones, it can seem sooo long 'til Santa Claus arrives! Have them make a big chain of paper links and give each link a number, from one to twenty-five. Every morning at breakfast, they can remove a link... and it's one day closer to Christmas!

Umm's Breakfast Casserole

Diane Cohen
The Woodlands, TX

My mom got this recipe with its funny name from an old church cookbook. For as long as I can remember, she has been making this delicious casserole on Christmas morning to share after all the gifts are opened. With only five ingredients, it comes together quickly...you don't even need to thaw the hashbrown patties!

8 small or 4 large frozen
　hashbrown patties
1 doz. eggs
2 c. milk

1 lb. ground pork sausage,
　browned and drained
2 c. shredded Cheddar cheese

Line the bottom of a greased 13"x9" baking pan with frozen hashbrown patties. Beat eggs and milk together; pour over hashbrowns. Bake, uncovered, at 350 degrees for 45 minutes. Remove from oven; sprinkle with sausage and cheese. Bake an additional 15 minutes, or until eggs are set. Let stand for 5 minutes before cutting. Serves 8 to 10.

A mug tree from the kitchen makes a clever holder for displaying several favorite Christmas ornaments.

Tapioca Fruit Delight

Lacey Wooten
Greenville, OH

This creamy, fruit-filled recipe is a favorite for brunch and potlucks because it makes so much. For a pretty presentation, spoon it into stemmed glasses and top with a dollop of whipped cream.

15-1/4 oz. can sliced pears, drained and juice reserved
16-oz. can apricot halves, drained and juice reserved
2 8-oz. cans pineapple chunks, drained and juice reserved
3-oz. pkg. cook & serve tapioca pudding mix
3-oz. pkg. cook & serve vanilla pudding mix
6-oz. jar maraschino cherries, drained
2 bananas, sliced

Pour reserved juices into a 4-cup measuring cup. Add enough water to equal 3 cups. Combine juice mixture and pudding mixes in a saucepan. Cook over medium heat, stirring constantly, until thickened; cool. Toss fruit together in a serving bowl. Pour pudding mixture over fruit; chill 4 to 6 hours or overnight. Mix in cherries and bananas just before serving. Serves 8 to 10.

Visit a local craft fair or two...it's sure to fill you with holiday cheer! They're a delightful source of handmade gifts and unique items that can't be found elsewhere. Treat yourself to hot cider and homemade cookies while you're shopping...what fun!

Zesty Orange Mini Muffins

Terri Deitrick
Newcastle, OK

These little muffins stir up quickly...their orange and lemon flavor can't be beat!

1/2 c. butter, softened	1 t. baking soda
1 c. sugar	3/4 c. buttermilk
2 eggs, beaten	1 c. golden raisins
2 c. all-purpose flour	1 c. chopped pecans

Blend butter and sugar together. Add eggs; beat for about 2 minutes. Sift flour and baking soda together. Add flour mixture alternately with buttermilk to butter mixture; stir in raisins and pecans. Fill greased mini muffin cups 3/4 full. Bake at 375 degrees for 15 minutes. Dip tops of warm muffins quickly into Citrus Glaze. Makes 3 dozen.

Citrus Glaze:

1/2 c. sugar	1-1/2 T. lemon juice
1/4 c. orange juice	1-1/2 t. lemon zest
2 T. orange zest	

Combine all ingredients; mix to a glaze consistency.

Surprise brunch guests with a muffin tree. Attach mini muffins to a tall styrofoam cone with toothpicks until the cone is completely covered. Try this with doughnut holes too...yummy!

Ham & Cheese Quiche

Melissa Rushing
Rogersville, MO

Great for breakfast or brunch...easy, quick and everyone loves it!

1-1/4 c. biscuit baking mix
1/4 c. butter, softened
2 T. boiling water
1 c. cooked ham, diced
1 c. shredded Cheddar or
    Colby Jack cheese

1/4 c. onion, diced
1-1/2 c. milk
3 eggs, beaten
1/2 t. salt
1/4 t. paprika

Stir baking mix and butter together until well blended. Add boiling water and stir to make a soft dough. Press into bottom and up sides of a greased 9" pie plate. Sprinkle ham, cheese and onion over dough. Whisk together milk, eggs, salt and paprika until well blended; pour into crust. Bake at 400 degrees for 35 to 40 minutes, until golden and center is set. Makes 6 to 8 servings.

Get ready to celebrate! Early in December, press the table linens and polish the silver. Later, as holiday meals and parties are being prepared, you can relax knowing these tasks are already done.

Amish Hashbrowns

Virginia Watson
Scranton, PA

*Real made-from-scratch hashbrowns! An Amish lady
shared this recipe with me one day when we were
visiting a country farmers' market.*

1/2 c. all-purpose flour
1/3 c. cornmeal
2 t. salt
pepper to taste
1 t. baking powder

5 c. potatoes, peeled
    and shredded
1 onion, minced
9 T. oil, divided
2 eggs, beaten

In a large bowl, mix together flour, cornmeal, salt, pepper and
baking powder. Add potatoes, onion, 5 tablespoons oil and eggs.
Mix until evenly blended; set aside. Heat remaining oil in a large
skillet over medium-high heat. Drop potato mixture into hot oil by
heaping tablespoonfuls, flattening slightly with a spatula. Cook
until golden on one side; turn and cook the other side until golden.
Makes 10.

Early in the holiday season, make a list of cookies to bake,
cards to write and gifts to buy...even Santa makes a list!
Post it on the fridge...you'll be able to check off each
item with satisfaction as it's completed.

Baked Spiced French Toast

James Bohner
Harrisburg, PA

This easy make-ahead recipe is my two sons' favorite Christmas tradition...mmm, so good! They eagerly wait for the sweet smell to wake them up.

12 slices cinnamon bread
6 eggs, beaten
1-1/2 c. milk
1-1/2 c. buttermilk
1 T. vanilla extract

1 t. pumpkin pie spice
1 T. cinnamon
Optional: blueberries, chopped
   walnuts or pecans

Arrange 6 bread slices in a greased 13"x9" baking pan; stack with remaining bread slices. Beat eggs, milk, buttermilk, vanilla and spices together; pour mixture over bread slices. Cover and refrigerate overnight. In the morning, prepare Syrup Topping and spoon over bread. Bake, uncovered, at 350 degrees for 45 to 50 minutes. Top with berries and nuts, as desired. Serves 6 to 8.

Syrup Topping:

3/4 c. butter, softened
1-1/2 c. brown sugar, packed

3 T. pancake syrup
1 t. cinnamon

Blend ingredients together.

When you want a warm, sweet treat on a busy morning, old-fashioned cinnamon toast is ready in a jiffy. Spread softened butter generously on one side of toasted bread, sprinkle with cinnamon-sugar and broil until hot and bubbly, one to two minutes. Perfect with a mug of hot cocoa!

Nan's Cinnamon Rolls

Ann Lyons
Ontario, Canada

This recipe was handed down to me nearly fifty years ago by my sister-in-law, who got the recipe from her mother, my mother-in-law. These cinnamon rolls are always the most requested by my family & friends at Christmastime.

3 c. all-purpose flour
2-1/2 t. baking powder
1 c. sugar, divided
2 eggs, beaten
1/2 c. milk

1/2 c. butter, softened
1 T. cinnamon
Optional: 16-oz. container
    cream cheese frosting

Sift flour and baking powder together; add 1/2 cup sugar. In a separate bowl, mix eggs, milk and butter. Add egg mixture to flour mixture; mix and knead together to form a soft dough. On a floured surface, roll out dough 1/4-inch thick into a 15-inch by 10-inch rectangle. In a small bowl, combine cinnamon and remaining sugar; sprinkle over dough. Roll up dough jelly-roll style; slice 1/2-inch thick. Place on ungreased baking sheets. Bake at 350 degrees for 15 to 20 minutes, or until golden. Spread warm rolls with frosting, if desired. Serve warm. Makes 2 dozen.

For your next brunch, fill sturdy diner-style mugs with ribbon-tied packets of spiced tea or hot cocoa. Add gift tags that read "Thinking warm thoughts of you this season." Set a mug at each place setting...they'll serve as both table decorations and take-home favors.

Pistachio Coffee Cake

Carol Barb
Johnstown, OH

It wouldn't be Christmas morning without a slice of this coffee cake to enjoy! The recipe has been shared so many times that now I make several cakes and send one home with guests. Everyone comments on how moist it is and how pretty for the holidays.

1 c. pecans, finely chopped
3/4 c. sugar
2 T. cinnamon
18-1/2 oz. pkg. yellow
   cake mix
3.4-oz. pkg. instant pistachio
   pudding mix

4 eggs, beaten
1 c. sour cream
3/4 c. orange juice or water
1/4 c. oil
1 t. vanilla extract

Mix together pecans, sugar and cinnamon; sprinkle 1/3 of mixture into a greased 10-cup Bundt® pan. Blend remaining ingredients together. Alternate layers of cake mixture with remaining nut mixture, for 3 total layers. Bake at 350 degrees for 40 to 50 minutes. Cool completely and remove from pan. Makes 10 to 12 servings.

Create a festive garland from Christmas cards to hang above the buffet. Simply punch a hole in the top corners of the cards and thread them onto a strand of ribbon.

Cozy Morning Brunch

Holiday Wassail

Tara Horton
Delaware, OH

*It's our family tradition to enjoy wassail while opening presents
Christmas morning. The citrus-spice aroma fills the house
and really puts us in the holiday mood!*

3 qts. apple juice
2-1/4 c. pineapple juice
2 c. orange juice

1/2 c. sugar
3-inch cinnamon stick
1 t. whole cloves

Combine all ingredients in a saucepan. Simmer, covered, over
medium-low heat for 30 minutes. Uncover; simmer for an additional
30 minutes. Strain; discard spices. Serves 10 to 12.

Christmas Brew

Mary Ann Dell
Phoenixville, PA

Perfect for a Christmas Eve get-together.

1/2 c. sugar
1/3 c. water
1/4 c. baking cocoa
1/4 t. cinnamon

10 c. hot brewed coffee
Garnish: milk, sugar,
whipped topping,
chocolate syrup

In a saucepan over medium heat, bring sugar, water, cocoa and
cinnamon to a boil. Boil for one minute, stirring frequently. Add to
brewed coffee; stir and serve immediately. Serve with milk and
sugar, dolloped with whipped topping and drizzled with chocolate
syrup. Makes 10 servings.

Bake some tasty cinnamon twists to serve alongside coffee!
Fold refrigerated bread stick dough in half and twist,
then roll generously in cinnamon-sugar and bake
as the package directs.

Country Sausage Gravy

Staci Meyers
Montezuma, GA

A family favorite year 'round!

1 lb. ground pork breakfast
  sausage
12-oz. can evaporated milk
1/4 c. butter, softened

2 to 3 T. all-purpose flour
pepper and garlic salt to taste
buttermilk biscuits, split

Brown sausage in a skillet over medium heat; drain. Stir in milk and
bring to a low simmer. Mix together butter and flour until smooth;
slowly stir into sausage mixture. Add seasonings to taste. Cook over
low heat for 5 minutes until thickened, stirring frequently. Serve
spooned over warm split biscuits. Serves 6.

Golden Drop Biscuits

Lisa Ann Panzino DiNunzio
Vineland, NJ

Guests will be so impressed, but these biscuits are simple to make.

2 c. all-purpose flour
4 t. baking powder
2 t. sugar
1/2 t. cream of tartar

1/2 t. salt
1/2 c. margarine
1 c. milk

Stir together flour, baking powder, sugar, cream of tartar and salt.
Cut in margarine with a pastry blender or 2 knives until mixture
resembles coarse crumbs. Add milk all at once; stir until dough sticks
together. Drop 2 tablespoonfuls of dough per biscuit onto a baking
sheet sprayed with non-stick vegetable spray. Bake at 450 degrees
for 10 to 12 minutes, until golden. Serve warm. Makes one dozen.

Mini Cheddar Soufflés

Zoe Bennett
Columbia, SC

Scrumptious on a holiday buffet spread.

3 T. butter
3 T. all-purpose flour
3/4 c. milk
3/4 c. shredded Cheddar cheese
1 T. Dijon mustard

4 slices bacon, crisply cooked
  and crumbled
4 eggs, separated
Optional: fresh parsley or
  chives, chopped

Melt butter in a saucepan over medium heat. Stir in flour; cook and stir for one minute. Gradually add milk; stir until well blended. Cook and stir until mixture comes to a boil. Remove from heat; stir in cheese until melted. Mix in mustard and bacon. Cool slightly. Stir in egg yolks one at a time; set aside. With an electric mixer on medium speed, beat egg whites until stiff but not dry, about 5 minutes. Gently fold into cheese mixture. Spoon into 12 lightly greased non-stick muffin cups or ramekins. Bake at 350 degrees for about 25 minutes, until puffed and set. Serve warm, garnished as desired. Makes 12.

Serve a zingy new fruit drink at breakfast. Mix equal parts chilled pomegranate juice, orange juice and lemon-lime soda or sparkling water. Pour into stemmed glasses over ice...so refreshing!

Crustless Broccoli Quiche

Tish Morgan
Dahlonega, GA

I created this recipe for all the low-carbers in my life to enjoy...it's been requested often at office potlucks. Slice it into generous squares to serve as a brunch dish with a fruit cup or into smaller squares for an appetizer.

8 eggs
16-oz. container cottage cheese
8-oz. pkg. shredded Cheddar
  cheese

2 16-oz. pkgs. frozen chopped
  broccoli, cooked and drained
salt and pepper to taste

In a large bowl, lightly beat eggs. Add remaining ingredients; mix well and transfer to a 9"x9" baking pan that has been sprayed with non-stick vegetable spray. Bake at 350 degrees for 45 to 60 minutes, until center is set and tests clean with a knife tip. Serve warm or at room temperature. Serves 4 to 6.

Turn cast-off holiday sweaters into whimsical Christmas stockings! Sweaters that are 100% wool can be felted (see page 205), while others can be backed with iron-on fusible interfacing. Cut out two simple stocking shapes and blanket-stitch together. Holiday handmade!

Sausage Breakfast Pie

Donna Lewis
Ostrander, OH

This recipe has been handed down through the years...we make it every Christmas morning. This can also be prepared ahead and refrigerated overnight, then baked in the morning. The peppers will rise to the top, adding a dash of Christmas color.

1 lb. ground pork breakfast
   sausage, browned and
   drained
9-inch pie crust
4 eggs, beaten
1 c. half-and-half

1-1/2 c. shredded Cheddar
   cheese
1/4 c. green pepper, diced
1/4 c. red pepper, diced
2 T. onion, chopped

Place browned sausage into unbaked pie crust; set aside. Whisk together remaining ingredients and pour over sausage. Bake at 375 degrees for 40 to 45 minutes. Serves 6.

Salt & pepper is a must with breakfast egg and potato dishes. Bring a little fun to the breakfast table with a pair of vintage-style "kissing" shakers!

Cranberry Christmas Canes

Laura Flores
Middletown, CT

My mother used this recipe for more than forty years...she always made them for our Christmas breakfast. We really looked forward to munching on these sweet pastries while we opened our gifts!

1 c. plus 1 to 2 t. milk, divided
4 c. all-purpose flour
1/4 c. sugar
1 t. salt
1 t. lemon zest
1 c. butter

1 env. active dry yeast
1/4 c. warm water
2 eggs, beaten
1/2 c. powdered sugar
1/4 t. vanilla extract

Heat one cup milk just to boiling; cool slightly. Combine flour, sugar, salt and lemon zest in a large bowl. Cut in butter with a pastry blender until mixture resembles coarse meal. Dissolve yeast in warm water, 100 to 115 degrees. Add yeast mixture, milk and eggs to flour mixture; combine lightly. Refrigerate for 2 hours to 2 days. At baking time, prepare Cranberry Filling; divide dough into 2 parts. On a floured surface, roll out half of dough into an 18-inch by 15-inch rectangle. Spread half of Cranberry Filling over dough. Fold rectangle into thirds, bringing both short edges over top of the center; press to seal. Slice rectangle into 15 strips. Holding both ends, twist each strip lightly in opposite directions; pinch ends. Place on a greased baking sheet; bend over tops to look like candy canes. Repeat with remaining dough and filling. Bake at 400 degrees for 10 to 15 minutes. Cool on wire racks. Mix powdered sugar with vanilla and remaining milk; frost pastries. Makes 2-1/2 dozen.

Cranberry Filling:

1-1/2 c. cranberries, finely
    chopped
1/2 c. sugar
1/2 c. raisins

1/3 c. honey
1/3 c. chopped pecans
1-1/2 t. orange zest

Combine all ingredients in a saucepan. Bring to a boil over medium heat. Cook for 5 minutes, stirring frequently. Cool.

SIMMERING
soups
& MORE

Creamy Tomato Tortellini Soup

Kathy Majeski
Pittsburgh, PA

My husband Rich and I celebrate Christmas with dear friends by having a progressive dinner. When it was my turn to do the soup course a few years ago, I experimented with tomato soup recipes for a few weeks before our dinner and this was the result. We love it... and everyone always wants the recipe!

4 10-3/4 oz. cans tomato soup
4-1/3 c. water
14-1/2 oz. can petite diced
   tomatoes
1 T. fresh basil, finely chopped,
   or 1 t. dried basil

Optional: salt and pepper
   to taste
1/2 c. fat-free half-and-half
16-oz. pkg. frozen cheese
   tortellini, cooked

In a large soup pot over medium heat, combine soup, water, tomatoes with juice and seasonings. Stir until well blended; bring to a simmer. Reduce heat and simmer 20 to 30 minutes. Stir in half-and-half; simmer over low heat an additional 5 minutes. Add cooked tortellini and heat through. Serves 8 to 10.

A vintage covered soup tureen does double duty
at a casual dinner of soup & sandwiches. It keeps the
soup hot and tasty while also serving as a centerpiece.

Pesto Chicken Paninis

Gretchen Brown
Forest Grove, OR

I created this recipe because I like pesto so much and also love hot sandwiches. They are such a good, quick lunch.

10-oz. can chicken, drained
1/4 c. prepared basil pesto
1/2 c. shredded mozzarella
   cheese

2 T. mayonnaise
8 slices whole-wheat bread

Mix together all ingredients except bread. Spread mixture on 4 slices of bread; top with remaining bread. Grill sandwiches in a panini grill or skillet over medium-high heat for about 3 minutes per side, until toasted and golden. Makes 4.

If you love to bake cookies and your best friend is a champ at wrapping, why not swap holiday talents? Afterwards, get together and share a tasty soup & sandwich lunch... a sure way to get into the holiday spirit!

Beef Stroganoff Sandwich

Carol Blankenship
Hamilton, OH

My family just loves this open-face sandwich! I always make it on special occasions like family get-togethers. It's a great recipe.

2 lbs. ground beef
1/2 c. onion, chopped
1/2 t. garlic powder
1 t. salt
1/2 t. pepper
1 loaf French bread, halved
   lengthwise

4 to 6 T. butter, softened
2 c. sour cream
2 tomatoes, diced
1 green pepper, diced
3 c. shredded Cheddar cheese

In a skillet over medium heat, brown ground beef and onion. Drain; stir in seasonings. Spread both halves of bread with butter; place butter-side up on an ungreased baking sheet. Remove skillet from heat; stir in sour cream. Spoon beef mixture onto bread; sprinkle with remaining ingredients. Bake at 350 degrees for 20 minutes, or until cheese is melted. If crisper bread is desired, bake a little longer. Slice into 3-inch portions to serve. Makes 6 servings.

Don't miss out on the season's first swirling snowflakes!
Bundle up the family and go on a winter hike, or take
everyone to a garden center or historic village where
horse-drawn carriage rides are given. Afterwards, everyone
can warm up with mugs of hot soup...what memories!

Herbed Chicken-Barley Soup

Janet Allen
Hauser, ID

Mmm...there's nothing better than homemade chicken soup! As soon as the temperature dips below freezing, I get out my big blue enamelware soup kettle and get a pot of this soup simmering.

3 to 4 lbs. chicken
8 c. water
1-1/2 c. carrots, diced
1 c. celery, diced
1/2 c. onion, chopped
1/2 c. pearled barley, uncooked

1 cube chicken bouillon
1/2 t. poultry seasoning
1/2 t. dried sage
1 t. salt
1/2 t. pepper
1 bay leaf

Place chicken and water in a large soup kettle. Simmer over medium heat until chicken is tender and juices run clear, about 25 to 40 minutes. Remove chicken and cool slightly, reserving broth in kettle. Allow broth to cool; skim off fat. When chicken is cool, cut into bite-size pieces, discarding bones and skin. Return chicken to broth in kettle along with remaining ingredients. Cover; simmer over low heat for at least one hour, until vegetables and barley are tender. Discard bay leaf before serving. Serves 6 to 8.

Bake a loaf of beer bread to serve with soup...easy!
Stir together 3 cups self-rising flour, 1/2 cup sugar and a
12-ounce bottle of beer or non-alcoholic beer. Pour
into a greased 9"x5" loaf pan. Bake for 35 minutes at
350 degrees. Drizzle 2 to 4 tablespoons melted butter over
the loaf and return to oven for 10 minutes. Scrumptious!

Curried Pumpkin Bisque

Joyce Teague
Providence, KY

*My family really enjoys this light soup during the winter. It is
my own recipe and makes an excellent first course for a Christmas
feast. It is very simple to prepare.*

1 onion, chopped
1/4 c. butter
2 T. all-purpose flour
1/2 t. curry powder
1/2 t. garlic salt
1/8 t. ground ginger

15-oz. can pumpkin
14-1/2 oz. can chicken broth
12-oz. can evaporated milk
Optional: red pepper flakes,
   whipping cream

In a skillet over medium heat, sauté onion in butter until onion is
translucent. Add flour and seasonings, stirring constantly. Slowly stir
in pumpkin and broth; simmer for 2 to 3 minutes. Add evaporated
milk; heat until bisque is simmering, but not yet boiling. Garnish
individual bowls of soup with a sprinkle of red pepper flakes or
a swirl of cream before serving, if desired. Serves 4 to 5.

Take along a thermos of creamy hot soup on an afternoon
of holiday errands...it's sure to give you a much-needed lift.

Connie's Pretzel Buns

Connie Mrazik
Saint Charles, MO

There is so much you can do with this recipe! You can coat them with butter after baking and sprinkle the tops with coarse salt or cinnamon-sugar. You can make mini sandwiches out of them too... cut when completely cool. But they're delicious just the way they are!

1 T. active dry yeast
2 T. sugar
1-1/2 t. salt
2-3/4 c. bread flour

3 T. butter, softened
1 c. warm water
6 c. cold water
5 t. baking soda

Place yeast, sugar, salt, flour and butter in a food processor. Pulse until butter is cut into dry ingredients. Add warm water, 110 to 115 degrees. Process until a soft dough forms, adding a little more water if needed. Dough should feel soft and elastic to the touch. Turn out into a greased bowl; cover and let rise until double. Punch down dough; form into golf ball-size buns. Press a finger almost, but not quite, through the center of each bun. Place buns on parchment paper-lined baking sheets; cover and let rise again until almost double. Heat cold water in a non-aluminum saucepan over high heat. Add baking soda; bring to a boil. Drop buns, 2 to 3 at a time, into boiling water. Boil for about 40 seconds on each side. Remove buns from water with a slotted spoon and return to parchment paper-lined baking sheets. Bake at 475 degrees for 8 to 12 minutes until golden, watching closely to avoid overbrowning. Cool buns on a wire rack. Makes 2 to 3 dozen.

A vintage holiday tea towel is a quick & easy wrap-up for small gifts. Place the gift in the center and bring the corners together. Secure with a length of ribbon and you're done!

Beefy Taco Pockets

Sherry Gordon
Arlington Heights, IL

*My kids love homemade tacos! They ask for tacos so often that
I thought I would give this recipe a try, just for a change.
Now these neat-to-eat pockets are a family favorite too.*

1 lb. ground beef
1-1/4 oz. pkg. taco seasoning
   mix
2/3 c. water
1-1/2 c. chunky salsa, divided

16.3-oz. can refrigerated jumbo
   biscuits
1 c. shredded Mexican-blend
   cheese blend, divided
Garnish: sour cream

Brown beef in a skillet over medium heat; drain. Stir in seasoning
mix, water and 1/2 cup salsa. Simmer for 2 to 3 minutes, until
thickened. Separate biscuits; flatten into 6-inch circles. Spoon beef
mixture and one tablespoon cheese onto each biscuit. Fold biscuits
in half over filling; press to seal well. Arrange on a lightly greased
baking sheet. Bake at 375 degrees for 9 to 14 minutes, until golden.
Garnish with remaining cheese, salsa and sour cream. Makes 8.

Chestnuts roasting on an open fire...try 'em for some
old-fashioned fun! Carefully cut an X in the top of the
nuts with a paring knife. Place them in a long-handled
popcorn popper and shake over hot coals for about
20 minutes. Or bake them in a shallow pan for 20 to
30 minutes at 425 degrees. Cool, then peel and enjoy.

Fresh Jalapeño Cornbread

Genia Kay Manning
Hamburg, AR

My church has a potluck once a month and I always take my
special cornbread. There's never any left to take home!

1/4 c. plus 1 T. oil, divided
1 c. plus 1 T. cornmeal, divided
1/2 t. salt
1/2 t. baking soda
1 c. buttermilk
2 eggs, beaten
8-3/4 oz. can corn, drained
2 jalapeño peppers, seeded and
   finely chopped
1/2 onion, finely chopped
8-oz. pkg. shredded Cheddar
   cheese

In a cast-iron skillet over medium-high heat, heat one tablespoon
oil. When skillet is hot, sprinkle with one tablespoon cornmeal. Mix
remaining ingredients; pour into hot skillet. Place skillet in oven.
Bake at 350 degrees for 45 minutes, or until set and golden. Cut
into wedges. Serves 8 to 12.

"A taste of home" is a thoughtful gift for a friend who has
moved away. Pack a container of a local food that she
misses...it could be jam, salsa, cheese or even your own
homemade cookies. Tuck in some picture postcards,
holiday clippings from a local newspaper and a snapshot
of your family holding a sign that says, "Merry Christmas
from back home!" She's sure to love it.

Chill-Chaser Chicken Soup

Cheryl McIntosh
Middletown, IN

My family requests this soup whenever they are under the weather,
especially on cold wintry days. It really warms the soul.

3 to 4-lb. chicken
2 stalks celery, halved
2 c. baby carrots, halved and
　divided
1 yellow onion, halved and
　divided
4 cloves garlic, divided
1 sprig fresh oregano
10 to 12 c. cold water

1 t. olive oil
1 jalapeño pepper, seeded and
　minced
1 T. fresh oregano, chopped
1-1/2 lbs. redskin potatoes,
　chopped
3 plum tomatoes, seeded and
　chopped
salt and pepper to taste

Place chicken into a large soup pot; add celery, one cup carrots,
1/2 onion, 2 garlic cloves and oregano sprig. Fill pot with cold water
2 inches above ingredients. Bring to a boil over high heat. Reduce
heat to medium; cover and simmer for one hour. Remove chicken
and set aside to cool. Strain broth into a large bowl, discarding
vegetables and oregano. Skim fat from broth and set aside. Add oil
to soup pot along with jalapeño, chopped oregano, remaining garlic
cloves, minced, and remaining onion, chopped. Cook over medium
heat until vegetables are just soft, about 5 minutes. Increase heat
to high; add reserved broth, potatoes and remaining carrots. When
broth boils, reduce heat to medium. Simmer until potatoes and
carrots are tender, about 15 minutes. Shred chicken into bite-size
pieces, discarding bones and skin. Add chicken and remaining
ingredients to soup; heat through. Makes 8 to 10 servings.

A "souper" gift for a new bride! Fill a roomy stockpot with
all the fixin's for a warming soup supper...a ladle, soup
seasonings and a big jar of your best warm-you-to-your-toes
soup! Be sure to include a copy of the recipe too.

Cheesy Garlic Pull-Apart Bread

Holly Snow
Everson, WA

If you don't have a bread machine, you can prepare this dough in a large bowl. Dissolve yeast in warm water, 110 to 115 degrees. Stir in remaining ingredients in the order listed and beat until smooth. Turn dough out onto a floured surface and proceed with the recipe.

1-1/2 t. active dry yeast	3 T. sugar
1/2 c. warm water	1-1/2 t. salt
4 t. butter, softened	3 c. bread flour
1/2 c. sour cream	

Heat water until very warm, about 110 to 115 degrees. Add water and remaining ingredients to a bread machine in order listed by bread machine manual. Select dough cycle. When cycle is completed, turn dough out onto a floured surface. Cover and let rise for 10 minutes. Pull dough apart by handfuls and dip in Cheesy Garlic Mixture. Place in a greased fluted pan. Cover and let rise for 45 minutes. Bake at 350 degrees for 30 minutes, until golden. Makes 10 to 12 servings.

Cheesy Garlic Mixture:

1/2 c. butter, melted	1-1/2 c. shredded Colby Jack
3 T. dried, minced onion	cheese
2 t. granulated garlic	

Mix all ingredients together.

Set a mini snowman at each person's place...so sweet! Simply attach two marshmallows together with a dab of frosting. Add a gumdrop hat and a tiny scarf cut from fruit leather, then use a toothpick to paint on frosting features.

Mini Butterscotch Drop Scones

Margaret Welder
Madrid, IA

My husband loves scones, so my recipe file has many different scone recipes, most of them rolled and cut into wedges. However, this one is a bit different because it is a drop scone and the butterscotch chips and nuts make it sweet.

2 c. all-purpose flour
1/2 c. brown sugar, packed
2 t. baking powder
1/4 t. salt
1/3 c. butter, softened
1 c. butterscotch chips

1/2 c. pecans, toasted
  and chopped
1 egg, beaten
2/3 c. whipping cream
1/2 t. vanilla extract
Optional: powdered sugar

Combine flour, brown sugar, baking powder and salt. Cut in butter with a pastry blender or 2 knives until fine crumbs form. Stir in chips and nuts. In a separate bowl, whisk together egg, cream and vanilla. Add to flour mixture, stirring just to moisten. Drop by rounded tablespoonfuls onto a parchment paper-lined baking sheet. Bake at 375 degrees for 12 to 15 minutes, until golden. Cool on a wire rack. Sprinkle with powdered sugar, if desired. Makes 3 dozen.

Make Mock Devonshire Cream to spoon onto warm scones...it's irresistible! Blend a 3-ounce package of cream cheese with one tablespoon sugar and 1/8 teaspoon salt. Stir in a cup of whipping cream. Beat with an electric mixer on high speed until stiff peaks form. Keep refrigerated.

Let-It-Snow Cocoa

Anjanette Kauffman
Seven Valleys, PA

I got this slow-cooker recipe from my sister one day when our kids were together sledding. It's very good and warms everyone up.

2 c. whipping cream
6 c. milk
1 t. vanilla extract

1 to 1-1/2 c. semi-sweet
    chocolate chips

Combine all ingredients in a slow cooker. Cover and cook on low setting for 2 to 2-1/2 hours. Stir well to blend before serving. Makes 10 servings.

Holiday Eggnog Bread

Summer Staib
Broomfield, CO

This was one of the first things that I ever made at age twelve. My family likes it very much during the holidays and I make it as long as the grocery store sells eggnog in the dairy section!

2 eggs, beaten
1 c. sugar
1 c. eggnog
1/2 c. butter, melted

1 t. vanilla extract
2-1/4 c. all-purpose flour
2 t. baking powder
2-1/4 t. ground nutmeg

In a large bowl, combine eggs, sugar, eggnog, melted butter and vanilla. Blend well. Add remaining ingredients; stir until moistened. Grease the bottom of a 9"x5" loaf pan; pour batter into pan. Bake at 350 degrees for 35 to 45 minutes, until a toothpick comes out clean. Cool completely before slicing. Makes one loaf.

Sounds of the season! String jingle bells on a sturdy wire, twist into a ring and hang on a doorknob.

James Family Toasty Sub

Shannon James
Georgetown, KY

With four children, we are always looking for budget-friendly meals that are healthful and well-balanced. When I first made this sandwich it was loved by the adults as much as the kids! Flavored loaves from the bakery are delicious, too. Serve with chips or potato salad on the side for a warm, hearty meal.

1 loaf French bread, halved lengthwise	1 lb. deli sliced turkey
	5 slices Swiss cheese
1/4 c. ranch salad dressing	1/4 c. cranberry sauce

Spread the cut side of half of the loaf with salad dressing. Layer with turkey and cheese slices. Place on a broiler pan and broil until cheese is melted and bubbly. Spread cranberry sauce on the cut side of other half of loaf. Close sandwich and slice. Makes 5 servings.

This year, why not have a homemade Christmas gift exchange? When family names are drawn, everyone agrees that all gifts are to be made by hand. Remember to start early! You may be pleasantly surprised at what clever ideas everyone comes up with.

Harvest Ham Chowder

Tomi Lessaris
Greenwood, IN

This recipe is one that all of my family really likes...it's simple enough for my daughters, Kaci, Lissi and Abbie, to make by themselves! Serve with crusty bread, crackers or cornbread.

2 T. oil
2 onions, diced
2 t. garlic, minced
1 green pepper, diced
4 potatoes, peeled and cubed
2 c. ham, cubed
1-1/2 to 2 c. frozen mixed
  vegetables

1 t. dried thyme
1 t. dried sage
salt and pepper to taste
4 to 6 c. water
2 12-oz. cans evaporated milk
1/4 c. butter, sliced
8-oz. pkg. favorite shredded
  cheese

Heat oil in a Dutch oven over medium-high heat; add onions, garlic, green pepper and potatoes. Sauté until onions are golden and potatoes are tender. Stir in frozen vegetables and seasonings; add just enough water to cover. Bring to a boil; lower heat and simmer for 15 minutes. Add evaporated milk, butter and cheese; cover and remove from heat. Let stand 5 minutes, until butter and cheese have melted. Serves 6 to 8.

Throw a spur-of-the-moment sledding party! Gather friends and neighbors to enjoy some snow fun together. Afterwards, head back home for mugs of hot cocoa or mulled cider in front of a cozy fire.

Stuffed Bread

Marlene Heaton
Gloucester, VA

My family always wants me to make this for our Christmas Eve dinner. The kids named it "Garbage Bread"...but it's delicious!

1 green pepper, quartered
1 red pepper, quartered
1 yellow pepper, quartered
1 onion, quartered
1 lb. ground beef, browned
  and drained
1 lb. ground pork sausage,
  browned and drained
1 T. garlic, minced
6-oz. can black olives, drained
  and diced

4-1/2 oz. can sliced
  mushrooms, drained
8-oz. pkg. shredded Pepper
  Jack cheese
8-oz. jar salsa
Optional: 1/4 c. pepperoni,
  chopped
1 loaf frozen bread dough,
  thawed

Place peppers and onion in a food processor and process until finely diced. Mix all ingredients except dough in a bowl; refrigerate 8 hours to overnight. On a floured surface, roll out thawed dough into a 15-inch by 10-inch rectangle. Spread chilled mixture over dough and roll up jelly-roll style. Place on a greased baking sheet. Bake at 350 degrees until golden, about 30 minutes. Slice to serve. Makes 8 servings.

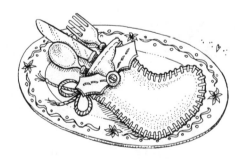

Tuck silverware into plush red mini Christmas stockings to lay on each guest's plate...how festive!

Crispy Butter Croutons

*Lynda Robson
Boston, MA*

Here in New England we're known for our thriftiness, so I enjoy turning day-old bread into crunchy croutons to sprinkle on soup or salad. I always cut the bread with a little star-shaped cookie cutter.

2 T. butter
1/2 t. dried parsley
1/8 t. paprika

1/8 t. garlic salt
1/8 t. pepper
2 slices day-old bread, cubed

Place butter in a microwave-safe medium baking dish. Microwave on high setting for about 25 seconds, until melted. Stir in seasonings. Add bread cubes; toss to coat. Microwave, uncovered, for 3 minutes, stirring once every minute until croutons are golden and crisp. Makes one cup.

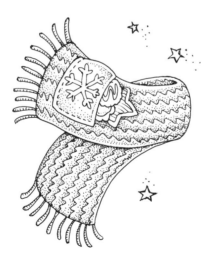

Give handknitted winter scarves as gifts...it's like giving a warm hug! Even beginning knitters can easily create nice-looking scarves. Choose a variegated yarn that makes its own stripes or use team colors...either way, your gift is sure to be a hit!

Meatball Potato Soup

Leslie Borelli
Pittsfield, ME

My mother-in-law used to serve this soup to my husband and he loves it, now I serve to my family. It is great on a nice cold day...we get a lot of them here in Maine!

32-oz. can beef broth
8 c. water
1 onion, halved and sliced
garlic powder, salt and pepper
   to taste

2 lbs. ground beef
6 potatoes, peeled and diced

Combine broth, water, onion and seasonings in a soup pot. Bring to a boil over medium-high heat; boil until onion is transparent. Form ground beef into small meatballs and drop into soup. Boil until meatballs are cooked through, about 35 to 40 minutes. Add potatoes for the last 20 minutes of cooking. Serves 8 to 10.

A delightful ice wreath for the front porch begins with items from the kitchen. Add about two inches of water to a fluted cake pan and freeze. Add a layer of fresh cranberries on top of the ice, fill mold with water and freeze again. Pop out of the pan and hang outdoors with a length of sturdy cord.

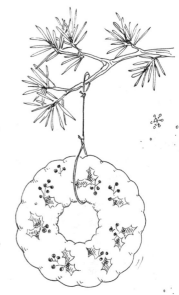

Turkey & Wild Rice Soup

JoAnn
Goooseberry Patch

Our favorite way to enjoy leftover holiday turkey.

1 onion, chopped
4-oz. can sliced mushrooms,
   drained
1 c. celery, diced
1 c. carrots, peeled and diced
1 c. frozen peas, thawed
2 T. butter

3 c. water
2 c. chicken broth
6-oz. pkg. long-grain and
   wild rice, uncooked
2 c. cooked turkey, diced
1 c. whipping cream

In a large saucepan over medium heat, sauté onion, mushrooms, celery and carrots in butter, until onion is tender. Add water, broth and rice with seasoning packet; bring to a boil. Reduce heat; simmer for 20 to 25 minutes, until rice is tender. Add turkey and peas; heat through. Stir in cream. Serves 6.

Leave a loaf of bread on the table after Christmas Eve
supper and you will have a full supply
until the next Christmas.

–Early American folklore

Hot Turkey Sandwiches

Beth Bundy
Long Prairie, MN

My mother-in-law gave me this slow-cooker recipe years ago...
my family loves it! I have substituted chicken for the turkey
and it was just as tasty.

1 c. onion, chopped
1-1/2 c. celery, chopped
3 T. butter
6 c. cooked turkey, shredded
10-3/4 oz. can cream of
   mushroom soup

3 c. pasteurized process cheese
   spread, cubed
15 sandwich buns, split

In a large saucepan over medium heat, sauté onion and celery in butter until tender. Add remaining ingredients except buns; mix well. Transfer to a slow cooker. Cover and cook on low setting for 3 to 4 hours. Serve on buns. Makes 15 servings.

Arrange a variety of mini breads, rolls and buns on a tiered cake stand alongside a variety of hot sandwich fillings and toppings. Guests will enjoy making different mini sandwiches to sample.

Homemade Chicken-Tomato Stew

Linda Hill
Athens, AL

This stew is good any time of the year.

3 to 4 boneless, skinless
   chicken breasts
5 c. water
2 15-oz. cans corn
28-oz. can diced tomatoes
2 T. chicken bouillon granules

1 onion, diced
2 potatoes, peeled and diced
10-3/4 oz. can tomato soup
2 T. hickory smoke-flavored
   cooking sauce
salt and pepper to taste

Place chicken and water in a soup pot. Simmer over medium heat
until chicken is tender. Remove chicken with a slotted spoon,
reserving broth. Shred chicken and return to broth. Add remaining
ingredients except salt and pepper; stir well. Simmer over low heat
for 45 minutes. Add salt and pepper to taste. Serves 6 to 8.

Tuck sweet family photos on wire picks into a festive
pine wreath...a super conversation starter for family &
friends as they visit over the holidays.

Vegetarian Chili

Gertrude Stevens
Sioux City, IA

On New Year's Day our family always enjoys oyster stew. However my sister-in-law doesn't like it, so one morning I was wondering what to make for her and came across this recipe. It was so good, everyone else had to have a bowl of it too! You will never miss the meat and won't even realize it isn't in the soup.

1 onion, chopped
1 green pepper, chopped
4 cloves garlic, minced
2 t. olive oil
14-1/2 oz. can reduced-sodium
   vegetable or chicken broth
16-oz. can kidney beans,
   drained and rinsed
16-oz. can fat-free refried
   beans

16-oz. can black beans,
   drained and rinsed
14-1/2 oz. can stewed
   tomatoes, chopped
3/4 c. salsa
2 t. chili powder
1/2 t. pepper
1/4 t. ground cumin
Optional: saltine crackers

In a large saucepan over medium heat, sauté onion, green pepper and garlic in oil until tender. Add remaining ingredients except crackers; mix well. Bring to a boil. Reduce heat; cover and simmer for 10 minutes. Serve with crackers, if desired. Makes 8 servings.

Share the Christmas spirit with a good winter deed...shovel the driveway and sidewalk for a neighbor. When you reach the doorstep, be sure to knock on the door and wish them a happy holiday!

Ham & Cheddar Cornbread

Arlene Smulski
Lyons, IL

This tasty cornbread is great for breakfast, lunch or brunch.
It goes well with soup, salad or a fruit cup.

2 8-1/2 oz. pkgs. cornbread
   mix
2/3 c. milk

2 eggs, beaten
1/3 lb. thinly sliced deli ham
6 slices Cheddar cheese

Combine dry cornbread mix, milk and eggs; mix well. Pour half of the batter into a 9"x9" baking pan sprayed with non-stick vegetable spray. Layer ham and cheese slices carefully over batter; spread remaining batter over cheese. Bake at 400 degrees for 20 to 25 minutes, until a toothpick inserted in the center comes out clean. Cut into squares; serve warm. Serves 6 to 8.

Instead of purchasing seasonal giftwrap, pick up a roll or two of white shelf paper. Stamp on a jolly design using red ink and whimsical rubber stamps...or let the kids do it! Top off wrapped gifts with bows of red bulky yarn... what a simple way to make any gift more special!

Slow-Cooked Hearty Pork Stew

Audrey Lett
Newark, DE

This is a super make-ahead recipe. Freeze stew and topping in separate containers, then thaw in the fridge two days ahead of serving.

1-1/2 lbs. boneless pork shoulder, cubed
1 lb. Kielbasa sausage, sliced
14-1/2 oz. can chicken broth
2 c. onion, chopped
6 carrots, peeled and thickly sliced
2 cloves garlic, minced

2 15-oz. cans cannellini beans, drained and rinsed
3 T. tomato paste
1 t. dried thyme
1/2 t. pepper
14-1/2 oz. can diced tomatoes, drained

In a slow cooker, combine all ingredients except tomatoes. Cover and cook on low setting for 8 to 10 hours, or on high setting for 4 to 5 hours. Stir in tomatoes; cover and cook an additional 10 minutes. Transfer stew to a greased shallow 3-quart casserole dish. Bake, covered, at 400 degrees for 30 minutes. Uncover; sprinkle with Crumb Topping. Return to oven for 15 to 20 minutes, or until topping is crisp and golden. Makes 8 servings.

Crumb Topping:

1-1/2 c. soft bread crumbs
1/4 c. fresh parsley, chopped

1/4 c. grated Parmesan cheese
2 T. olive oil

Toss all ingredients together.

WARM & WELCOMING
Suppers

FOR POP

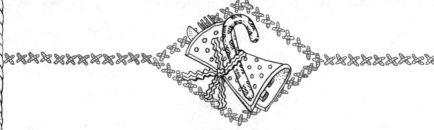

Dawn's Homemade Meatloaf

Dawn Hester
Buckhead, GA

*My best friend Erica and I came up with this recipe one night
for supper. Now my family is happy to have meatloaf
at least once a week!*

1-1/2 lbs. ground beef
1 onion, chopped
1 egg, beaten
2 8-oz. cans tomato sauce,
   divided
1 c. soft bread crumbs

1/2 t. salt
1/4 t. pepper
1/4 c. dark brown sugar,
   packed
2 T. dried parsley
1 T. Worcestershire sauce

Combine ground beef, onion, egg, one can tomato sauce, bread
crumbs, salt and pepper; mix well. Form into 8 mini meatloaves
and place in a 13"x9" baking pan sprayed with non-stick vegetable
spray. Bake, uncovered, at 400 degrees for 25 minutes. Drain any
excess fat. Combine remaining ingredients with second can of
tomato sauce; spoon over meatloaves. Reduce oven temperature
to 350 degrees; bake an additional 20 to 25 minutes. Serves 8.

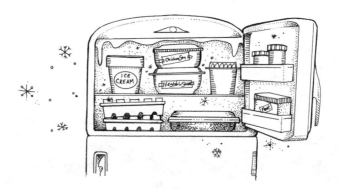

December is packed with things to do, so take it easy with
simple, hearty meals. Make double batches of family
favorites like chili or Sloppy Joes early in the holiday season
and freeze half to heat & eat later. What a time-saver!

Special Baked Chicken

Laurel Perry
Loganville, GA

Even my choosy kids love this quick & easy dish!

4 to 6 boneless, skinless
   chicken breasts
18-1/2 oz. can French onion
   soup

1/2 c. sour cream
1/2 T. Worcestershire sauce
1/2 t. dried thyme
salt and pepper to taste

Place chicken in a greased 13"x9" baking pan; set aside. Combine remaining ingredients in a saucepan over medium-low heat. Cook, stirring occasionally, until well blended. Pour mixture over chicken. Cover; bake at 350 degrees for 50 minutes, or until chicken juices run clear. Serves 4 to 6.

Creamed Sweet Peas

Susi Dickinson
Prentice, WI

When fresh peas aren't in season, you can substitute a thawed 16-ounce package of frozen baby sweet peas.

1 T. all-purpose flour
1/4 c. sugar
2/3 c. milk

2 c. peas
1/4 t. pepper

In a saucepan over medium heat, combine flour, sugar and milk; mix well. Add peas and pepper; bring to a boil. Reduce heat; simmer for 10 to 12 minutes, or until peas are heated through and sauce has thickened. Makes 4 to 6 servings.

Don't wait until Christmas Day to use your festive holiday dishes...use them all season long for a daily dash of cheer!

Oh-So-Easy Pot Roast Dinner

Nadine Hogrefe
Bend, OR

The fastest pot roast in town! This has been my go-to recipe for over thirty years. Just toss everything into the slow cooker in the morning and voilà! A great no-fuss dinner that's packed with juicy flavor.

2 to 3-lb. boneless beef chuck
  roast
3 to 5 cloves garlic, halved
  lengthwise
3 to 5 T. all-purpose flour
salt and pepper to taste

2 T. canola oil
1 onion, sliced
6 carrots, peeled and halved
4 to 6 new redskin potatoes
10-1/2 oz. can beef consommé

Cut slits into the top and bottom of roast with a knife tip. Insert garlic clove halves into slits. Coat roast with flour; sprinkle with salt and pepper. Heat oil in a skillet over medium-high heat. Add roast and brown on all sides. Remove roast to a slow cooker; cover with sliced onion. Arrange carrots and potatoes around roast. Pour broth over roast. Cover and cook on high setting for 5 to 6 hours. Serves 4 to 6.

Christmas is the family time, the good time of the year.

–Samuel Johnson

Buttery Herbed Noodles

Claire Bertram
Lexington, KY

A super-easy side that goes well with almost any meal. For even more flavor, I'll toss in a chicken bouillon cube as the noodles are boiling.

3 T. butter
1 clove garlic, minced
1/4 t. dill weed
1/4 t. dried thyme

1/4 t. salt
8-oz. pkg. medium egg
   noodles, cooked

Melt butter in a skillet over medium-low heat. Add garlic and cook for one to 2 minutes; stir in seasonings. Add cooked noodles to butter mixture; toss to coat well. Makes 4 servings.

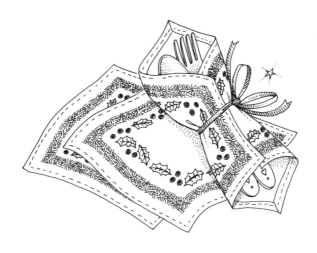

Quick, easy handmade napkins...there are so many
cute holiday fabrics that you'll want to make lots!
Cut 4, 18-inch squares from a yard of cotton fabric. Turn
in each edge 1/8 inch and press, then turn and press again.
Stitch close to the folded edge...pretty and useful!

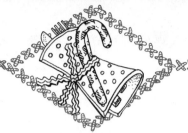

Judy's Kickin' Chicken

Judy Davis
Muskogee, OK

With just four ingredients, this is the easiest chicken recipe ever...and it's so good! This is wonderful served with rice, but we also like it with quick chicken stuffing mix and fresh green beans.

1/4 c. butter
8 chicken thighs

2 c. light soy sauce, divided
1 c. water

Melt butter in a large skillet over medium heat. Add chicken; cook until golden on both sides. Drizzle chicken with half the soy sauce; continue cooking for 5 minutes. Turn chicken; cover with remaining soy sauce. Add water to skillet; reduce heat to medium-low. Simmer until chicken juices run clear and sauce is caramelized, about 20 minutes, adding a little more water if needed. Serves 4 to 6.

Make a living rosemary wreath. Insert a circle of wire
in a potted rosemary plant and use thread to train stems
onto the wire. In just a few weeks, new growth will fill
out the shape of the wreath. Enjoy its fragrance in the
kitchen window or tie on some tiny bows and
give it to a favorite cook.

Speedy Skillet Pecan Rice

Linda Belon
Wintersville, OH

Turn this tasty side dish into a main...just sauté some chopped chicken along with the veggies. A quick stir in the skillet, a couple of boil-in bags of rice and dinner is served!

1 onion, chopped
1/2 red pepper, chopped
1 c. mushrooms, sliced
2 T. oil
1 clove garlic, minced
2 3-1/2 oz. boil-in bags
  white rice, cooked

1 t. Cajun seasoning
1/4 t. salt
1/2 t. pepper
Garnish: 3 T. chopped pecans,
  toasted

In a skillet over medium heat, sauté onion, red pepper and mushrooms in oil for about 5 minutes, until tender. Add garlic; sauté for 2 minutes. Stir in cooked rice and seasonings; sprinkle with pecans. Makes 4 servings.

If your house has no mantel for hanging up stockings filled with goodies, try this! Attach Shaker pegs to a wooden plank, one for each member of the family. The rest of the year, it'll be a handy place for hanging jackets and sweaters.

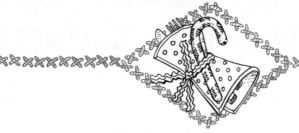

Gramp's Goulash

Megan Kreplin
Coxsackie, NY

This recipe has been in my family for a very long time...my mother remembers her grandmother making this dish. It's a very fast one-pot meal. Add some crusty bread and a salad and you have a delicious healthy meal. It's a good make-ahead meal too...prepare the beef sauce at your convenience and refrigerate it for up to 3 days, then rewarm and serve over freshly cooked macaroni.

1 onion, cut into strips
1 green pepper, cut into strips
2 to 3 T. water
1 lb. ground beef
2 14-1/2 oz. cans diced
   tomatoes

salt and pepper to taste
16-oz. pkg. elbow macaroni,
   cooked

In a skillet over medium heat, sauté onion and pepper in water until tender and water cooks off. Add ground beef; cook until browned. Stir in tomatoes, breaking them up a little with a spoon. Stir in salt and pepper. Reduce heat to low; cover and simmer at least one hour. To serve, spoon over cooked macaroni. Makes 4 to 6 servings.

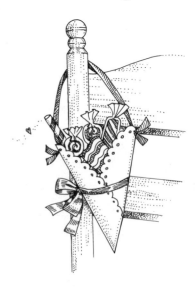

Fill Victorian-style paper cones with old-fashioned hard candies and tiny toys. Hang from chair backs with ribbons for a charming welcome at a holiday meal for family & friends.

Mom's Green Beans & Bacon

Cindy DeCarlo
Sullivan, MO

My mother always simmered these green beans all day on the stovetop. I've turned it into an easy slow-cooker recipe...it's still the most scrumptious way to enjoy green beans!

4 14-1/2 oz. cans green beans, drained
2 14-oz. cans chicken broth with roasted garlic
1 onion, cut into 6 wedges
1/2 lb. bacon, diced and partially cooked, drippings reserved
salt and pepper to taste

Place all ingredients in a slow cooker; stir. Cover and cook on low setting for 8 hours, or on high setting for 5 hours. Serves 6.

Consider sending postcards instead of ordinary Christmas cards. They're fun to send, don't take long to write and cost less to mail. Pick up some nostalgic old-time reproductions or make your own postcards using scrapbooking supplies. Either way, they're sure to be remembered!

Crisp Celery-Pear Salad

Stephanie Mayer
Portsmouth, VA

A wonderful cool-weather salad...makes a delicious lunch too.

4 stalks celery, halved
   lengthwise
2 T. cider vinegar
2 T. honey
1/4 t. salt

2 red pears, cored and diced
8-oz. pkg. white Cheddar
   cheese, diced
pepper to taste
1/2 c. chopped pecans, toasted

Place celery in a bowl of ice water for 15 minutes. Drain celery and pat dry; slice 1/2-inch thick. Whisk vinegar, honey and salt together in a serving bowl. Add pears; gently stir to coat. Add celery and remaining ingredients; stir to combine. Serve at room temperature. If desired, make up to 2 hours ahead, reserving pecans. Chill; stir in pecans at serving time. Makes 6 servings.

A gift card is anything but ordinary when tucked into a
handmade felt envelope. Simply cut two small rectangles
of felt with pinking shears and glue or sew together
on three sides. Add the recipient's name in glitter
paint...how special!

Big Butterflies & Mushrooms

Isolda Crockett
Mossville, IL

I'm half Italian, and my fondest memory is sitting in Nana's big kitchen while she talked, cooked and watered her flowers. She was so sweet and kind. When I make her recipes, it is like she is still there with me.

1/2 c. butter
5 shallots, chopped
1-1/2 lbs. mushrooms, chopped
1/2 c. chicken broth
1/2 t. salt
1/4 t. cayenne pepper
16-oz. pkg. large bowtie pasta, cooked
1/2 c. grated Romano cheese

Melt butter in a skillet over medium heat. Add shallots and cook until soft. Add mushrooms and broth to skillet. Lower heat and simmer for 4 to 5 minutes, stirring often. Add seasonings; stir well and cook for 5 more minutes. Place cooked pasta in a warmed large serving bowl; add cheese and toss. Pour mushroom sauce over pasta and gently toss to coat well. Makes 6 servings.

Have the kids build a snowman at Grandma & Grandpa's house while they're out Christmas shopping. Remember to add a woolly scarf, hat and mittens...hand-me-downs would be perfect. What a thoughtful way to share some winter fun!

Mashed Potato Casserole

Weda Mosellie
Phillipsburg, NJ

*With crisp bread crumbs and savory salami, this hearty
potato casserole is just a little different!*

1/2 c. butter, divided
1/2 c. dry bread crumbs
4 c. mashed potatoes
1/4 lb. deli sliced Italian salami,
   prosciutto or ham, chopped

2 green onions, finely chopped
salt and pepper to taste
Optional: 2 to 3 T. milk

Use 2 to 3 teaspoons of butter to grease an 8"x8" baking pan. Coat
bottom and sides of pan with bread crumbs and set aside. Combine
remaining ingredients except milk in a bowl. Mix, thinning with a
little milk if too thick. Transfer mixture to prepared pan; dot with
remaining butter. Bake, uncovered, at 375 degrees for 35 minutes,
until heated through and golden. Serves 6.

There are always so many tempting treats during the
holidays. Lighten things up by keeping a bowl filled
with shiny apples or pears. They'll double as a pretty
centerpiece and as a healthy, crunchy-sweet snack.

Louisiana Chicken

Susan Maurer
Dahlgren, IL

*My sister, Nancy, gave me this super-easy recipe...it's become
a weeknight favorite with my family.*

2 slices bacon
1/2 c. onion, chopped
1 green pepper, sliced
1/8 t. dried thyme

10-3/4 oz. can tomato soup
1/2 c. water
1-1/2 c. cooked chicken, diced
cooked rice

In a skillet over medium-high heat, cook bacon until crisp. Remove
bacon and drain, reserving drippings in skillet. Reduce heat to
medium. Add onion, pepper and thyme to drippings; cook until
tender. Stir in soup, water and chicken. Heat through, stirring
occasionally. Serve over cooked rice, garnished with crumbled
bacon. Serves 4.

Snowy paper-white narcissus flowers
are a hint of spring in wintertime...they
make super gifts too! Place bulbs
pointed-side up in water-filled bulb
vases and set in a sunny window.
In about six weeks you'll have
cheerful blooms.

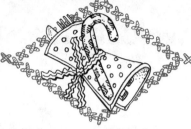

Morgan's Crabby Mac & Cheese

Judy Roberts
Lakeville, MA

When my five-year-old granddaughter, Morgan, invited me to her school's potluck, I asked, what can I bring? She said a main dish. I wanted to make a new dish that both kids and adults would like, then I thought, everyone loves macaroni & cheese! Here is my "new" mac & cheese recipe.

16-oz. pkg. small macaroni shells, cooked
8-oz. pkg. frozen imitation crabmeat, thawed and coarsely chopped
1 red pepper, diced
1 onion, diced
1 t. olive oil

16-oz. pkg. pasteurized process cheese spread
3/4 to 1 c. milk
1 t. dill weed
1/2 t. cayenne pepper
3/4 c. mayonnaise-type salad dressing

Place macaroni and crabmeat in a large bowl and set aside. In a saucepan over medium heat, sauté red pepper and onion in oil until tender. Reduce heat to low. Add remaining ingredients except salad dressing, stirring constantly until cheese is melted. Pour into macaroni mixture. Add salad dressing; mix well. Transfer to an ungreased 1-1/2 quart casserole dish. Bake, uncovered, at 300 degrees for 20 minutes, until hot and bubbly. Makes 4 to 6 servings.

Whenever a dinner guest asks, "How can I help?" be ready with an answer! Whether it's setting the table, filling glasses with ice or even bringing their special dessert, friends are usually happy to pitch in.

Quick & Easy Baked Fish

Cheri Emery
Quincy, IL

A light, healthy dish for those days when you've already enjoyed one-too-many Christmas cookies!

4 frozen cod or tilapia fillets,
   thawed
1/4 c. dry bread crumbs

1/4 t. lemon-pepper seasoning

Arrange fish in a lightly greased 13"x9" baking pan. Combine bread crumbs and seasoning in a small bowl; spoon over fish. Bake, uncovered, at 400 degrees for 15 to 20 minutes, until fish flakes easily with a fork. Makes 4 servings.

Sesame Asparagus

Marlene Darnell
Newport Beach, CA

The sauce is tasty with fresh broccoli too.

1 lb. asparagus, trimmed and
   cut into 1-inch pieces
1 T. oil
1 T. soy sauce
1 T. sugar

2 t. rice wine or cider vinegar
2 t. sesame seed, toasted
Garnish: 4 to 5 slices bacon
   crisply cooked and crumbled

Fill a medium saucepan with water; bring to a boil over medium heat. Add asparagus and cook just until tender, about 5 minutes. Drain; keep warm. In a small saucepan over medium heat, combine oil, soy sauce, sugar and vinegar; bring to a boil. Cook and stir for one minute, until sugar dissolves. Pour sauce over asparagus and toss to mix; sprinkle with sesame seed. Top with bacon. Serves 4 to 6.

Quick & easy napkin rings! Cut empty paper towel tubes into 2-inch sections and cover them with giftwrap.

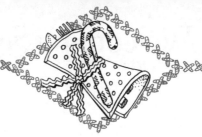

Carrots Vichy

Denise Webb
Galveston, IN

*Even the kids will love this yummy dish. Lemon-lime soda
can be substituted for the club soda.*

1-1/2 lbs. carrots, peeled and
    sliced 1/2-inch thick
1-1/2 c. club soda
2 T. sugar

6 T. margarine, sliced
salt and pepper to taste
Garnish: 2 T. fresh parsley,
    minced

Place carrots, club soda, sugar and margarine in a saucepan. Cover
and cook over medium-low heat for 20 to 30 minutes, until carrots
are tender. Remove carrots with a slotted spoon to a serving dish;
cover to keep warm. Increase heat to high; boil cooking liquid until
reduced in volume and slightly thickened. Pour over carrots. Add
salt and pepper to taste; sprinkle with parsley. Serves 4 to 6.

For whimsical giftwrap, there are all kinds of papers to
try...the Sunday comics, shiny magazine pages, old road
maps, even foreign-language newspapers. Just tie on a
bow...you'll be adding some fun to the gift, while using
items that would otherwise be tossed out.

Yam-a-Dandy

Judith Griffith
Greensville, SC

One taste and you'll agree...these sweet potatoes are just dandy!

29-oz. can sweet potatoes,
   drained and mashed
1/2 c. sugar
2 eggs, beaten

1/2 c. butter, melted
1 c. light corn syrup
Optional: chopped walnuts
   or pecans

Combine all ingredients except nuts; mix well. Pour into a greased
2-quart casserole dish. Bake, uncovered, at 350 degrees for
30 minutes. Garnish with nuts, if desired. Serves 4.

Old-Time Pickled Peaches

Lisa Sett
Thousand Oaks, CA

*A simple and delicious recipe that's a tradition in our house.
My family has served these for generations...they're a "must" year
'round at both holiday dinners and summer cookouts.*

2 15-1/4 oz. cans peach halves,
   drained and juice reserved
3 to 6 4-inch cinnamon sticks,
   broken in half

1 t. whole cloves
2 T. white vinegar
1/2 c. sugar

Pour reserved juice into a large saucepan over medium heat. Heat
to boiling; add remaining ingredients except peaches. Simmer
5 minutes. Add peaches; simmer an additional 5 minutes. Remove
from heat and allow to cool. Discard spices. Chill before serving.
Serves 6 to 8.

Becky's Artichoke-Rice Salad

Becky Zetnick
Mansfield, TX

I don't recall where I got this recipe, but each time I serve this salad someone requests it...easy, simple and yummy! Most of the ingredients are pantry staples too, which is convenient.

6.2-oz. pkg. fried rice-flavored
    rice vermicelli mix, cooked
10-oz. can white chicken,
    drained
8-oz. can sliced water
    chestnuts, drained
6-oz. jar marinated artichoke
    hearts, drained, chopped
    and marinade reserved

6-oz. can black olives, drained
    and sliced
1/4 c. mayonnaise
Optional: 4 green onions, sliced

Combine all ingredients including reserved marinade in a large serving bowl. Mix well. May be served warm or chilled. Serves 6.

Create a whimsical one-of-a-kind wreath from old Christmas cards. Start with a wreath-size circle of foam core or heavy cardboard. Clip out images like angels or Santas from cards to cover the wreath. Glue in place with craft glue, overlapping some and adding on tiny bows, pom-poms or other accents as you go. How clever!

Orange Chops & Rice Tango

Diane Billert
Rockford, IL

In 1990, I was vacationing in Maui when a dress-shop owner shared this recipe with me. It's been a favorite ever since...the pork chops fixed this way are really delicious and moist.

4 to 6 pork chops, sliced
    1/2-inch thick
1/4 t. ground ginger
1/4 t. pepper
3 t. chicken bouillon granules,
    divided
1 to 2 T. oil
1 onion, thinly sliced

2 c. water
1 c. orange juice
1/4 c. catsup
2 T. brown sugar, packed
2 t. dry mustard
1/2 t. salt
1 c. long-cooking rice,
    uncooked

Season pork chops with ginger, pepper and one teaspoon bouillon granules. In a large skillet over medium heat, brown pork chops in oil on both sides. Remove pork chops from skillet; drain. Stir in onion and sauté lightly. Stir in remaining bouillon and other ingredients except rice; bring to a boil. Stir in rice and place pork chops on top. Cover; lower heat and simmer 30 minutes. Serves 4 to 6.

Host a Christmas gift-tag making party! Invite friends to bring scrapbooking supplies, rick rack, glitter, old Christmas cards...any kinds of leftover craft materials. You provide plain cardstock, craft glue, scissors and some yummy refreshments. Everyone will have a ball mixing & matching to make brand-new creations.

Slow-Cooker 16-Bean Stew

Debbie Blundi
Kunkletown, PA

I created this stew one snowy day in December. My husband, the ladies at my Bible study and our weekly Sunday luncheon guests at church all gave it rave reviews, so it's a keeper at our house!

16-oz. pkg. 16-bean soup mix
26-oz. jar pasta sauce
24-oz. jar salsa
1-1/4 oz. pkg. taco seasoning
  mix

1 onion, diced
Optional: 1 lb. boneless pork
  ribs, cubed
3 to 4 c. cooked brown or
  white rice

The night before, place bean soup mix in a large pot; add enough water to cover by 4 inches. In the morning, drain and rinse beans. Combine with remaining ingredients except rice in a 7-quart slow cooker. Cover and cook on low setting for 10 hours or on high for 6 hours, until beans are tender. Stir after 4 hours; stir once or twice during rest of cooking time. Thirty minutes before serving, stir in enough cooked rice to absorb any broth. Cover; let stand 15 to 30 minutes before serving. Serves 10 to 15.

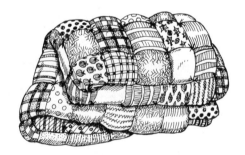

Put on a slow-cooker dinner and have a quilting bee!
Get together with family & friends to craft an
extra-special quilt for one lucky recipient...a new bride,
a new baby, Mom & Dad's 50th anniversary. With many
hands, the quilt will be done in no time at all!

Spicy Cabbage-Apple Slaw

Edie DeSpain
Logan, VT

We really like the crunchiness of this salad that comes from the cabbage, apples, celery and walnuts...yum! It goes really well with baked ham, grilled sausages and other pork dishes.

2 c. shredded green and red
   cabbage mix
2 c. Red Delicious apples, cored
   and chopped
1/2 c. celery, chopped
2 T. walnuts, chopped and
   toasted

2 T. golden raisins
1/2 c. plain yogurt
2 T. apple juice
1 T. honey
1/2 t. cinnamon

In a large serving bowl, combine cabbage mix, apples, celery, nuts and raisins; toss well. Combine remaining ingredients in a small bowl, stirring well. Pour yogurt mixture over cabbage mixture; toss well. Cover and chill for at least 30 minutes before serving. Makes 8 servings.

Be sure to have a holiday family time one night a week in December. Read holiday books together, watch holiday movie classics or just enjoy mugs of hot cocoa by the twinkling lights of the Christmas tree. You'll be making memories that will last for years.

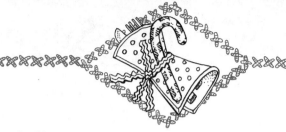

Taco Skillet Dinner

Gretchen Brown
Forest Grove, OR

This is a good, quick dinner idea that we all enjoy. Sometimes we spoon it into flour tortillas to eat like a soft taco.

1 lb. ground beef
2 c. water
1-1/4 oz. pkg. taco seasoning
  mix
2 c. instant rice, uncooked
1/4 lb. pasteurized process
  cheese spread, cubed

1 c. shredded Cheddar cheese
1/2 c. sliced black olives,
  drained
2 c. lettuce, shredded
2 c. tomatoes, chopped
Garnish: sour cream, salsa

Brown beef in a skillet over medium heat; drain. Add water and seasoning mix; stir. Bring to a boil. Stir in rice and cheese spread. Sprinkle with shredded cheese; cover and reduce heat to low. Simmer for 5 minutes. Top with olives, lettuce and tomatoes. Garnish as desired with sour cream and salsa. Serves 4.

Invite friends to join you for a favorite weeknight skillet or slow-cooker meal in December...a meal shared with friends doesn't need to be fancy. After all, it's friendship that makes it special!

Last-Minute Lasagna

Lisa Sett
Thousand Oaks, CA

*This recipe is a huge time-saver over made-from-scratch lasagna...
even better, it's scrumptious enough to serve to company.*

26-oz. jar pasta sauce, divided
20-oz. pkg. refrigerated cheese
  ravioli, divided
10-oz. pkg. frozen chopped
  spinach, thawed, drained
  and divided

8-oz. pkg. shredded mozzarella
  cheese, divided
1/2 c. grated Parmesan cheese,
  divided

Spread 1/2 cup pasta sauce in the bottom of an ungreased
9"x9" baking pan. Layer half the ravioli, half the spinach, half of
the cheeses and 1/3 of remaining sauce. Repeat layers, ending
with cheeses. Cover with aluminum foil. Bake at 350 degrees for
25 minutes. Uncover; bake an additional 10 minutes. Serves 6.

Tie up festive bundles of flatware for your holiday potluck.
Wrap silverware in a red cloth napkin and tie with
gold cording. Tuck in a sprig of fresh pine and place in
a wicker basket at the end of the buffet line.

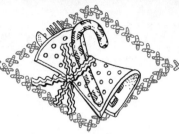

Speedy Chinese Noodles

Kay Marone
Des Moines, IA

A great side dish for teriyaki chicken.

1/4 c. oil
6 cloves garlic, chopped
1/8 to 1/4 t. red pepper flakes
8-oz. pkg. thin spaghetti,
   cooked

2 to 4 T. soy sauce
Garnish: chopped green onion

Heat oil in a skillet over medium-high heat. Add garlic and red pepper flakes; cook and stir for 2 minutes. Add cooked spaghetti and toss well. Stir in soy sauce and heat through. Garnish servings with chopped onion. Makes 6 servings.

The sweetest little ornaments to hang on the Christmas tree or on an evergreen wreath. Paint tiny terra-cotta flowerpots red with acrylic paint, then hang a jingle bell inside with yarn.

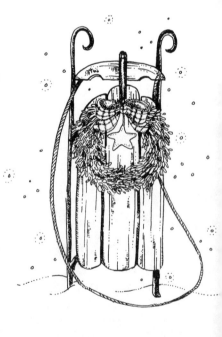

FARMHOUSE
Christmas Dinner

Holiday Pork Loin

Patricia Ferraiolo
East Haven, GA

We tried this scrumptious slow-cooker recipe with cranberries, squash and apples for the first time this past Christmas. It was such a big hit that we are including it again in this year's menu.

1 c. apple cider or apple juice
2-lb. boneless pork loin
1/2 t. salt
1/4 t. pepper
3 Granny Smith apples, cored,
    peeled and sliced
1 butternut squash, peeled
    and cubed
12-oz. pkg. cranberries
2 to 3 T. brown sugar, packed
1/2 t. cinnamon
1/2 t. nutmeg
1/4 t. dried sage

Pour apple cider or juice into a skillet over medium-high heat. When liquid is hot, add pork loin and sear on all sides. Sprinkle salt and pepper over pork; remove to a slow cooker. Drizzle skillet drippings over pork. Combine apples, squash and cranberries and sprinkle with remaining ingredients. Stir to combine ingredients and place around pork in slow cooker. Cover and cook on low for 5 to 6 hours. Remove pork loin from slow cooker and let stand for 10 to 15 minutes. Slice into 1/2-inch slices. Top with apple mixture and serve. Serves 6 to 8.

Keep the Christmas dinner menu simple, familiar and yummy. You may even want to ask your family ahead of time what dishes or foods are "special" to them. It's a day for tradition and comfort... and you'll be a more relaxed hostess too.

Christmas
Dinner Menu

Holiday Pork Loin
Grandma's String
Beans
Carrot Casserole
Egg Nog Pie

Grandma's Swiss String Beans

Audrey Zukowski
Clintondale, NY

My grandmother always made this bean dish for Christmas. When she could no longer do the cooking, my aunt took over, then my mother, then me. Now my children enjoy it at Christmas too. You can use fresh, canned or frozen green beans.

1/4 c. plus 2 T. butter, divided
1/2 c. dry bread crumbs
2 T. all-purpose flour
1 T. onion, minced
1 t. sugar
1 t. salt
1/4 t. pepper
1 c. sour cream
4 c. green beans, trimmed and
    thinly sliced lengthwise
2 c. shredded Swiss cheese

Melt butter in a large saucepan over low heat. Toss 2 tablespoons butter with bread crumbs; set aside for topping. Blend flour, onion, sugar, salt and pepper into remaining butter in saucepan. Add sour cream and stir until smooth. Increase heat to medium; cook and stir until thick and bubbly. Fold in beans; transfer to a greased 13"x9" baking pan. Sprinkle with cheese and bread crumb mixture. Bake, uncovered, at 400 degrees for 20 to 25 minutes. Makes 6 servings.

For a pretty yet super-speedy centerpiece, wrap chunky pillar candles in a length of glittery wide ribbon and fasten with double-stick tape. A great way to use all those snips of extra ribbon too!

Savory Roast Turkey Breast

Jennie Gist
Gooseberry Patch

This roast turkey is delicious, yet so simple to make!

5-1/2 to 6-lb. bone-in turkey
   breast
1/2 c. butter, sliced
1/4 c. lemon juice
2 T. soy sauce
1 T. dried sage

1 t. dried thyme
1 t. dried marjoram
1/4 t. pepper
2 T. green onions, finely
   chopped

Place turkey breast in an ungreased shallow roasting pan. Insert a meat thermometer into thickest part; set aside. Combine remaining ingredients in a small saucepan over medium-low heat. Bring to a boil; mix well and remove from heat. Brush butter mixture over turkey breast. Roast, uncovered, at 325 degrees for 1-1/2 to 2 hours, or until thermometer reads 165 degrees, basting with butter mixture every 30 minutes. Remove turkey breast to a platter; cover lightly to keep warm. Let stand for about 10 minutes before slicing. Serves 10 to 12.

Homemade pan gravy is delicious and easy to make. Remove the roast turkey to a platter. Set the roaster with pan juices over medium heat. Shake together 1/4 cup cold water and 1/4 cup cornstarch in a small jar and pour into the roaster. Cook and stir until gravy comes to a boil and thickens, 5 to 10 minutes. Add salt and pepper to taste, and it's ready to serve.

Roasted Garlic Mashed Potatoes

Janet Allen
Hauser, ID

Here in Idaho we eat potatoes so often that I'm always looking for new ways to make them extra flavorful...this is a real winner! Be sure to start the garlic spread ahead of time.

2 lbs. potatoes, peeled
   and cubed
1/4 c. butter, sliced

1/4 c. sour cream
salt and pepper to taste
1 to 2 T. milk

Cover potatoes with water in a saucepan. Cook over medium-high heat until potatoes are tender, 15 to 20 minutes; drain. Place potatoes in a large bowl; add Roasted Garlic Spread and remaining ingredients except milk. Beat with an electric mixer on medium speed to desired smoothness, adding milk as needed. Serves 4.

Roasted Garlic Spread:

1 bulb garlic, cloves separated   1 T. olive oil

Toss unpeeled garlic cloves in oil. Wrap tightly in a small square of aluminum foil and place in a small casserole dish. Bake at 350 degrees for 35 to 45 minutes, until soft. Cool slightly. Press out softened garlic into a bowl; mash with a fork.

Set up a Christmas corner... a quiet place with favorite holiday books, a basket for incoming Christmas cards & letters...perhaps even soft music playing nearby and a jigsaw puzzle to work. It'll be a peaceful retreat where family members can relax and reflect on the meaning of the season.

Feliz Navidad Casserole

Tracee Cummins
Amarillo, TX

More than twenty years ago, my husband and I were newlyweds attending college in Lubbock, Texas. I clipped the original recipe for this casserole out of the local newspaper. I've changed it over the years to include our family's favorite ingredients. It's a real winner!

1-1/2 lbs. ground beef
1 onion, chopped
10-3/4 oz. can cream of
   chicken soup
10-oz. can red enchilada sauce
4-oz. can diced green chiles
2 t. ground cumin

1/2 t. salt
1/2 t. pepper
3 c. shredded Mexican-blend
   or Monterey Jack cheese,
   divided
10 8-inch flour tortillas

Brown beef and onion in a large skillet over medium heat; drain. Stir in remaining ingredients except cheese and tortillas; simmer for 10 minutes. Spread 1/3 of meat sauce in a greased 13"x9" baking pan. Sprinkle with one cup of cheese. Add a layer of tortillas, tearing tortillas to fit pan and completely covering the sauce and cheese. Repeat layers, ending with remaining sauce and cheese. Bake, uncovered, at 350 degrees for 20 minutes, or until bubbly and cheese is melted. Serves 8.

Pair a gift of special-event tickets with a small themed item. Tuck football tickets inside a warm handknit cap... wrap up tickets to a movie with a few squares of homemade fudge...add a pretty scarf to a gift of concert tickets. It's sure to be appreciated!

Mexican Black-Eyed Peas

Hope Davenport
Portland, TX

*We always have black-eyed peas for good luck on New Year's Day.
I like them spiced up a bit, as in this recipe from
my husband's grandma.*

16-oz. pkg. dried black-eyed
   peas
1 lb. ground pork sausage
1 onion, finely chopped
18-oz. can whole tomatoes
1/2 c. water

2-1/2 T. celery, finely chopped
2 T. sugar
2-1/2 T. chili powder
2 T. garlic salt
1/4 t. pepper

Place dried peas in a Dutch oven; add water to cover by 2 inches.
Soak for 6 to 8 hours, or overnight. Brown sausage in a skillet over
medium heat; drain. Add onion and cook until tender. Drain peas;
stir into sausage mixture. Add tomatoes with juice and remaining
ingredients. Bring to a boil. Cover; reduce heat and simmer for
1-1/2 hours, stirring occasionally and adding more water as
necessary. Makes 6 servings.

Be a family of cheerful givers! Look around the house for
gently used clothing, toys and household items to give to
charity. Or bake cookies together to take to a nursing
home or community shelter. Take a family trip to deliver
your donations...it's sure to get you in the holiday spirit.

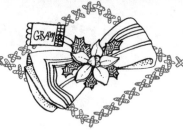

Best-Ever Italian Bread

Denise Mainville
Huber Heights, OH

One word sums up this recipe...yummy! This is a must
with all our Italian dinners.

1 loaf Italian bread
1/2 c. grated Parmesan cheese
1/3 c. mayonnaise
1/4 t. dried basil

1/4 t. garlic powder
1/8 t. dried oregano
1/8 t. garlic salt

Slice loaf into 12 slices without cutting through the bottom. Place on an ungreased baking sheet. Combine remaining ingredients in a small bowl and mix well. Spread mixture between slices and over top of loaf. Bake at 400 degrees until golden, about 12 to 14 minutes. Serves 6.

It was a handmade Christmas. The tree came from down in the grove, and on it were many paper ornaments made by my cousins. ... There were popcorn balls from corn planted on the sunny slope next to the watermelons, paper horns with homemade candy and apples from the orchard. ... And there were real candles burning with real flames.

–Paul Engle

Special Baked Lasagna

Gretchen Brown
Forest Grove, OR

My mother-in-law has made this recipe for years and it is always so delicious. At my husband's request, she's even served it alongside the roast turkey on Christmas Day!

1 lb. ground beef, browned
   and drained
14-1/2 oz. can diced tomatoes
2 6-oz. cans tomato paste
1 c. water
1 clove garlic, pressed
1 T. dried basil
3 T. dried parsley, divided
2-1/2 t. salt, divided

3 c. cottage cheese
1/2 c. grated Parmesan cheese
2 eggs, beaten
1/2 t. pepper
16-oz. pkg. lasagna noodles,
   uncooked
2 8-oz. pkgs. shredded
   mozzarella cheese

In a large bowl, prepare sauce mixture by combining ground beef, tomatoes with juice, tomato paste, water, garlic, basil, one tablespoon parsley and 1-1/2 teaspoons salt; set aside. In a separate bowl, prepare cheese mixture by stirring together cottage cheese, Parmesan cheese, eggs, pepper and remaining parsley and salt. Spoon 1/3 of sauce mixture into an ungreased deep 13"x9" baking pan. Layer with half each of uncooked noodles, sauce mixture, cheese mixture and mozzarella; repeat layers. Make sure noodles are completely covered by sauce. Cover pan with aluminum foil. Bake at 375 degrees for 45 minutes. Uncover; bake an additional 15 minutes, until bubbly and heated through. Makes 12 servings.

Start a sweet new tradition at your holiday dinner...hand out paper star cut-outs and have each person write down what they're happiest for since last Christmas.

Slow-Cooked Applesauce

Mary Talalay
Lutherville, MD

As a blended Jewish and Christian family, we've created many traditions for our special family. I first made this applesauce for Thanksgiving, but Hanukkah also includes apples as part of the tradition, so it's perfect for us. This is yummy over vanilla ice cream, with gingersnaps or all by itself!

1/2 c. water
8 to 10 Granny Smith apples,
   cored, peeled and cubed

1 to 2 T. lemon juice
1 to 2 T. dark brown sugar,
   packed

Pour water into a slow cooker. Add apples; drizzle with lemon juice. Cover and cook on low setting for 6 hours, stirring after 2 hours. Applesauce should be a chunky consistency after 6 hours. If a smoother consistency is preferred, spoon applesauce into a food processor and purée as desired. Stir in brown sugar to taste. Makes 8 servings.

Slow cookers are oh-so-handy helpers during the holidays. Free up space in the oven and on the stovetop by filling them with scalloped potatoes, savory bread stuffing or corn pudding. They're super for keeping spiced cider or cranberry punch simmering or cheesy appetizers piping-hot too.

Black Cherry Cranberry Salad

Leigh Ellen Eades
Summersville, WV

I remember my mother making this salad for every Thanksgiving and Christmas when I was a child. Now, when planning my own holiday meals, this salad is always at the top of the menu!

8-oz. can crushed pineapple
1/4 c. water
3-oz. pkg. black cherry
   gelatin mix
16-oz. can whole-berry
   cranberry sauce

1 c. celery, chopped
1 c. chopped walnuts
1/4 c. lemon juice

In a saucepan over medium heat, mix undrained pineapple and water. Heat to boiling; add gelatin mix and stir until gelatin is dissolved. Add remaining ingredients and stir well. Transfer to a 6-cup serving dish. Chill in refrigerator for 4 hours, or until firm. Makes 8 servings.

For a festive garnish on cranberry salads, use a mini cookie cutter to cut star or flower shapes from fresh orange peels.

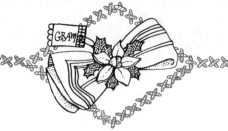

Brown Sugar-Glazed Ham

Jo Ann
Gooseberry Patch

Guests will love this tender baked ham with its fruity brown sugar glaze. Dress it up by scoring the unbaked ham in a diamond pattern and pressing a whole clove into each diamond.

10-lb. fully-cooked bone-in
   ham
1-1/2 c. water
1-1/4 c. dark brown sugar,
   packed
1/3 c. pineapple juice

1/3 c. honey
2 T. Dijon mustard
1 T. orange juice
2 t. orange zest
1/4 t. ground cloves

Place ham in an ungreased large roasting pan; pour water into pan and set aside. In a saucepan over medium heat, whisk together remaining ingredients. Bring to a boil; reduce heat to low and simmer for 5 to 10 minutes. Brush ham with glaze; tent lightly with aluminum foil. Bake at 325 degrees for 2 hours; uncover. Brush ham with glaze. Bake, uncovered, for an additional 30 minutes, brushing with glaze every 10 minutes. Let stand for 15 to 20 minutes; slice to serve. Makes 12 to 15 servings.

Gather up little mittens or gloves that the children
have outgrown...they make such a sweet decoration for
a front-door wreath. Add a bow made of a child-size
knitted scarf...charming!

Twice-Baked Potato Casserole

*Sandy Roy
Crestwood, KY*

This hearty casserole is loaded with an irresistible combination of bacon, sour cream, cheese and green onions...yum! I like to leave the potatoes unpeeled to add real baked potato flavor.

6 baking potatoes, baked, cubed and divided
1/4 t. salt
1/4 t. pepper
1 lb. turkey bacon, crisply cooked and crumbled

3 c. sour cream, divided
2 c. shredded mozzarella cheese, divided
2 c. shredded Cheddar cheese, divided
Garnish: 2 green onions, sliced

Place half the potato cubes in a greased 13"x9" baking pan. Sprinkle with salt, pepper and bacon; top with half each of the sour cream and cheeses. Repeat layers. Bake, uncovered, at 350 degrees for about 20 minutes, until cheese is melted. Sprinkle with green onions before serving. Serves 6 to 8.

Need a candlelit centerpiece in a hurry? Clear glass hurricanes, punched-tin lanterns or simple candlestands all look festive when arranged together in a group of similar items. Take a look around the house and see what you can find!

Captain Harris's Seafood Quiche

Angie Biggin
Lyons, IL

This luxuriously rich quiche is best served in small portions to savor each and every bite! Captain Harris was a famous steamboat captain in Galena, Illinois in the 1800s. This quiche was served at a bed & breakfast in Galena.

8-oz. pkg. shredded Swiss
  cheese, divided
9-inch deep-dish pie crust
6-oz. can crabmeat, drained
  and flaked
10-oz. pkg. frozen chopped
  spinach, thawed and
  drained

1 c. cooked small or medium
  shrimp
6 eggs, beaten
1 c. whipping cream
3/4 c. half-and-half
1 T. fresh dill, chopped
1/8 t. cayenne pepper

Place half the cheese in pie crust. Top with crab, spinach, shrimp and remaining cheese. Whisk together remaining ingredients; pour over cheese. Bake at 350 degrees for 15 minutes. Reduce temperature to 300 degrees. Bake an additional 30 to 40 minutes longer, until a knife tip inserted into center comes out clean. Let stand 10 minutes before cutting into wedges. Serves 6 to 8.

Start a Christmas album and add to it every year...a family photo taken in front of the tree, the children's letters to Santa, notes on favorite gifts received and special visitors. Display it where family & friends can enjoy looking at it... sure to make for many smiles over the years!

Homemade Crescent Rolls

Karen Rissler
McAlisterville, PA

These buttery made-from-scratch rolls are a big hit with my in-laws every Christmas!

1 T. active dry yeast
1/2 c. plus 1 t. sugar, divided
1/2 c. warm water
1 c. butter, melted

2 eggs, beaten
1 t. salt
4 c. all-purpose flour
3/4 c. milk

In a large bowl, mix yeast and one teaspoon sugar with very warm water, about 110 to 115 degrees; let stand until dissolved. Add remaining sugar and other ingredients; mix well. Cover and refrigerate for 5 hours to overnight. Divide dough into 3 to 4 balls. On a lightly floured surface, roll out each ball into a 10-inch round and cut into 12 triangles. Roll up triangles starting at the wide end; form into crescents. Arrange crescents on baking sheets that have been lightly sprayed with non-stick vegetable spray. Cover and let rise until double in size, about one hour. Bake at 350 degrees for 10 minutes until golden, watching closely to avoid browning. Makes 3 to 4 dozen.

Planning a big holiday menu packed with homemade goodness? Be sure to include items that are easily made ahead. Many side-dish casseroles, breads and even desserts can be prepared and frozen as much as one to two months in advance, then thawed overnight and warmed as needed.

Sweet-and-Sour Brisket

Beth Shaeffer
Greenwood, IN

This is a great alternative to the traditional Sunday pot roast. It tastes even better the next day, sliced and made into sandwiches! This brisket can easily be prepared in a slow cooker, if you prefer. Cook it on low setting for 6 to 8 hours.

2 T. oil
4-lb. beef brisket
28-oz. can crushed tomatoes
1 c. catsup

3/4 c. brown sugar, packed
1/2 c. balsamic vinegar
1.35-oz. pkg. onion soup mix

Heat oil in a large oven-proof saucepan over medium heat. Brown brisket on both sides; drain. Mix remaining ingredients; pour mixture over brisket. If necessary, add a little water so that brisket is half covered by liquid. Cover and bake at 350 degrees for 3 to 4 hours, until tender. Makes 6 to 8 servings.

Wouldn't doting grandparents love to receive a grandchild's best artwork in a sweet frame? Paint a simple frame in a color that goes well with the picture, then glue on wooden alphabet tiles to spell out the child's name. A gift that's sure to be cherished!

Susan's Famous Carrots

Kathleen Niedbala
Pawcatuck, CT

My mom has made this delectable dish for as long as I can remember. My siblings and I request it for every special meal. There are never any leftovers...it's always the first dish to go!

2 onions, chopped
3/4 c. butter, melted and
    divided
1/4 c. all-purpose flour
1/4 t. dry mustard
1 t. celery salt
1 t. salt
1/8 t. pepper

2 c. milk
2 16-oz. pkgs. frozen sliced
    carrots, cooked and drained
3/4 lb. white Cheddar cheese,
    sliced
2 sleeves round buttery
    crackers, finely crumbled

In a skillet over medium heat, sauté onions in 1/4 cup butter until translucent. Stir in flour and cook for one minute. Add mustard, celery salt, salt and pepper; slowly add milk. Reduce heat to low. Cook, stirring constantly, until mixture is thickened and smooth. In a lightly greased 2-1/2 quart casserole dish, layer carrots alternately with cheese slices, making 3 to 4 layers and ending with carrots. Pour sauce over top. Toss cracker crumbs with remaining butter; sprinkle over casserole. Bake, uncovered, at 350 degrees for 30 minutes, or until golden on top. Serves 8.

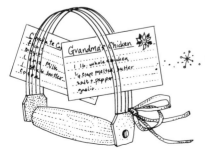

A gift of a casserole dish or a small kitchen appliance that's anything but ordinary! Tuck in several handwritten recipe cards featuring several yummy ways to use the gift...perhaps even a couple of jars of special spices or seasonings.

Honey Sweet Potatoes

Barbara Bargdill
Gooseberry Patch

*We like this sweet & simple recipe better than the usual
marshmallow-topped holiday sweet potatoes.*

3 lbs. sweet potatoes, peeled
   and cubed
1/4 c. butter

1/4 c. honey
2 t. lemon juice
salt and pepper to taste

In a lightly greased 13"x9" baking pan, arrange sweet potatoes in
a single layer; set aside. In a small saucepan, stir together butter,
honey and lemon juice over low heat until butter melts. Drizzle over
sweet potatoes; toss well to coat. Sprinkle with salt and pepper.
Bake, uncovered, at 350 degrees until fork-tender, about 30 to
40 minutes, stirring after 15 minutes. Serves 6.

If guests will be coming & going at different times on
Christmas Day, serve a casual buffet instead of a sit-down
dinner. With a spread of sliced baked ham or roast beef, a
choice of breads and sandwich fixin's, warm sides waiting
in slow cookers and a luscious dessert tray, guests will
happily serve themselves at their own pace.

Maple-Baked Acorn Squash

Lorrie Haskell
Lyndeborough, NH

Here in New Hampshire we make our own maple syrup and use it in many dishes. This is a flavorful family favorite that's easily doubled or tripled as needed.

1 acorn squash, halved and
  seeded
1/2 c. maple syrup, divided

2 t. butter, diced and divided
salt and pepper to taste

Fill an ungreased 9"x9" baking pan with 1/2 inch of water. Place squash halves in pan, cut-side up. Pour 1/4 cup of syrup into each squash half. Dot each with one teaspoon of butter; sprinkle with salt and pepper. Cover pan with aluminum foil. Bake at 350 degrees for about 45 to 50 minutes, until squash is tender. Serves 2.

Use favorite cookie cutters for all kinds of crafting!
Trace around them onto brightly colored paper for
placecards and gift tags...add a dash of glitter for sparkle.
Or make simple ornaments...trace a cookie cutter
onto doubled felt and cut out, then blanket-stitch
together and stuff lightly...so cute!

Easy "Rotisserie" Chicken

Patti Walker
Mocksville, NC

*This slow-cooked chicken is so juicy it will melt in your mouth.
Even small kids just love it! I developed this recipe during fall sports
season, when we were always rushing after school to tennis and
football practice. Add some pasta or rice and a salad for a nice
meal between all of your after-school activities.*

5 to 7-lb. roasting chicken
1 lemon, sliced
Optional: 1 sprig fresh
   rosemary or thyme
2 T. butter, melted

1 t. garlic powder
1/2 t. poultry seasoning
1 t. onion powder
1 t. paprika
pepper to taste

Roll 2 to 3 pieces of aluminum foil into balls; place in a large oval
slow cooker. Pat chicken dry with paper towels. Place lemon slices
inside chicken along with herb sprig, if using. Loosen the skin on
breast; rub melted butter and other seasonings under loosened skin.
Place on top of foil balls, breast-side up. Do not add any liquid to
slow cooker. Cover and cook on low setting for 8 hours, or on high
setting for 4 hours. Chicken will be very tender; use a wide spatula
or lifter to remove carefully from slow cooker. If a crisper skin is
desired, place chicken on a baking sheet and broil the top briefly,
until crisp and golden. Serves 4 to 6.

Ask Grandmother & Grandfather to tell you about
their earliest childhood Christmas memories...be sure
to capture these sweet stories on video.

Spiced Apple-Cranberry Sauce

Jackie Smulski
Lyons, IL

A zingy sauce that's just a little different from the usual cranberry sauce...and so easy to make! It's a great time-saver during the holidays, since it can be kept covered and refrigerated for a week.

2 Granny Smith apples, cored, peeled and finely chopped
3/4 c. sugar
1/2 c. cranberry juice cocktail

2 T. balsamic vinegar
4-inch cinnamon stick
12-oz. pkg. cranberries

In a saucepan, combine all ingredients except cranberries. Bring to a boil over medium heat. Stir in cranberries; reduce heat and simmer for 8 to 10 minutes. Remove from heat; discard cinnamon stick. Cover and chill before serving. Serves 4 to 6.

Create a special desk calendar for a good friend. Select a plain calendar at an office supplies store, then add favorite quotes and sayings she would enjoy. Decorate with scrapbooking supplies for a one-of-a-kind gift she's sure to love.

Spicy Citrus Salad

Diane Hixon
Niceville, FL

I was experimenting in the kitchen when I tossed this salad together. It was a hit at Thanksgiving dinner. The spiciness is just right...very refreshing and not overpowering.

1/2 t. cayenne pepper
1 t. paprika
1/2 t. garlic powder
3 T. olive oil
1 T. red wine vinegar
1/3 c. fresh parsley, chopped

3 seedless oranges, peeled
   and sectioned
1/4 to 1/3 c. pitted black olives,
   halved lengthwise
6 c. mixed salad greens, torn

Whisk together spices, oil and vinegar in a serving bowl. Stir in parsley, oranges and olives. Cover and refrigerate for one hour. Toss with salad greens and serve immediately. Serves 6.

Celebrate the first day of winter by taking a family nature walk and collect some pine cones to make a treat for the birds. Tie a hanging string to the top of each pine cone, then spread with peanut butter mixed with cornmeal and roll in bird seed. The birds will love it!

Mini Butterscotch Drop Scones, page 54

Cherry Streusel Coffee Cake, page 22

Christmas Brew, page 37

Mrs. Claus' Christmas Bread, page 23

Spinach & Mozzarella Quiche, page 25

Country Sausage Gravy, page 38

Fresh Jalapeño Cornbread, page 51

Turkey & Wild Rice Soup, page 61

Crispy Butter Croutons, page 59

Harvest Ham Chowder, page 57

Spicy Cabbage-Apple Slaw, page 87

Curried Pumpkin Bisque, page 48

Beef Stroganoff Sandwich, page 46

Sesame Asparagus, page 81

Savory Roast Turkey Breast, page 94

Yam-a-Dandy, page 83

Mini Cheddar Soufflés, page 39

Mocha Pudding Cake, page 134

Red Velvet Christmas Cake, page 129

Peanutty Chocolate Clusters, page 173

Tossed Salad & Cider Dressing

Tina Wright
Atlanta, GA

With three kinds of apple, the creamy dressing makes this salad perfect for a chilly-weather dinner.

2 c. fresh spinach, torn
2 c. romaine lettuce, torn

1 c. iceberg lettuce, torn

Toss together spinach and lettuces in a salad bowl. Drizzle with Cider Dressing; toss well and serve immediately. Makes 6 servings.

Cider Dressing:

1/4 c. frozen apple juice
    concentrate, thawed
3 T. sour cream
3 T. water
2 T. cider vinegar
2 T. fresh parsley, chopped

2 T. apple, cored, peeled and
    finely shredded
1 T. Dijon mustard
1/4 t. salt
1/8 t. pepper

Whisk together all ingredients. Keep refrigerated; shake well before using.

Fill a large basket with all the groceries for a holiday dinner...seasonal two-for-one sales will help make this budget-friendly. Have the kids make a sign saying "Happy Holidays from Our Family to Yours" and deliver the basket to a neighborhood charity. A sure way to remember what Christmas is all about!

Almond Rice Pilaf

Cathy Forbes
Hutchinson, KS

*A tasty change from potatoes that's especially good with chicken.
My husband sometimes nibbles on the seasoned almonds
before I have a chance to put them on the rice!*

3 c. water
3 c. instant rice, uncooked
5 T. plus 1 to 2 t. margarine,
  divided
1 T. chicken bouillon granules
1/2 c. onion, chopped

2 T. soy sauce
1/2 c. sliced almonds
1 T. ranch salad dressing mix
  or 1 t. garlic salt and
  herb blend

In a saucepan over high heat, bring water to a boil. Remove from heat; add rice, 3 tablespoons margarine and bouillon. Stir; place lid on pan and let stand for 5 minutes. In a skillet over medium heat, sauté onion in 2 tablespoons margarine until tender. Fluff prepared rice with a fork; stir into onion mixture in skillet. Add soy sauce and stir well; heat through. Remove rice mixture to a serving bowl; cover to keep warm. In the same skillet, toast almonds in remaining margarine and dressing mix or herb blend, until lightly golden. Sprinkle almonds over rice mixture and serve. Makes 6 servings.

Host a tree-trimming party! Invite all the cousins,
aunts & uncles for a merry time hanging ornaments
and twining garland...even set up a table of craft materials
so guests can make their own. Afterwards, share holiday
plans over a simple supper...such fun!

Raspberry-Glazed Salmon

Rebecca Barna
Blairsville, PA

*If you're looking for an alternative to all the roast beef,
ham and turkey during the holidays, or just want a lighter meal,
this is a delicious choice.*

1 lb. salmon, cut into
    4 to 5 fillets
1/4 c. butter, melted
1/2 c. brown sugar, packed

3 T. fresh dill, chopped
1/4 to 1/2 c. raspberry
    vinaigrette salad dressing

Place salmon fillets in an ungreased 2-quart casserole dish; set aside. For the marinade, whisk together remaining ingredients. Reserve 1/4 cup of marinade; drizzle remaining marinade over salmon. Cover and refrigerate for at least one hour, turning twice. Drain and discard marinade from casserole dish. Cover dish with aluminum foil; bake at 350 degrees for 20 to 25 minutes. Uncover; drizzle 2 tablespoons of reserved marinade over salmon and bake an additional 5 minutes, until salmon flakes easily with a fork. Place salmon on a serving platter and drizzle with remaining marinade. Serves 4 to 5.

Let the children write and illustrate the annual family Christmas letter! Far-away friends are sure to be charmed and you'll get a fresh glimpse into what events and activities really mattered to the kids this year.

Favorite Sausage-Apple Stuffing

Vickie
Gooseberry Patch

Pork sausage, onion, apple and two kinds of stuffing...yummy! This recipe has all the good country flavors, yet is ready in 30 minutes. It makes a great stuffing for baked butterflied pork chops.

1/2 lb. ground pork sausage
1 onion, coarsely chopped
1 stalk celery, coarsely chopped
1/8 t. pepper

14-1/2 oz. can chicken broth
1 apple, cored and chopped
2 c. herb-flavored stuffing mix
2 c. cornbread stuffing mix

In a large saucepan over medium heat, brown sausage with onion, celery and pepper. Drain; stir in broth and apple. Bring to a boil; reduce heat to low. Cover and simmer for 5 minutes, or until apple is tender. Add stuffing mixes; toss lightly to moisten well. Cover again; let stand for 5 minutes before serving. Serves 4 to 6.

Make dried apple slices for country-style Christmas crafting. Slice apples thinly, soak them in lemon juice for 20 minutes and pat dry. Spread slices on a baking sheet and bake at 200 degrees for 2 to 3 hours. String them with cinnamon sticks and star anise on strips of homespun for sweet-smelling swags or toss several slices into a bowl of potpourri.

Sweet Potato Soufflé

Jessica Silva
East Berlin, CT

Last year I served my very first family Christmas dinner. I knew I had to "wow" everyone with their favorite dishes, but wanted to make them mine. Instead of a traditional sweet potato recipe, I made this soufflé. They all loved it...I'm sure you will too!

3 sweet potatoes, peeled,
    cooked and mashed
1/2 c. butter, softened
1 c. sugar
2 eggs, beaten
1/2 c. evaporated milk

2 t. vanilla extract
1/2 t. salt
10-1/2 oz. pkg. mini
    marshmallows
1/4 c. brown sugar, packed

Combine all ingredients except marshmallows and brown sugar. Mix well and place in a greased 1-1/2 quart casserole dish. Bake, uncovered, at 325 degrees for 25 minutes. Arrange marshmallows on top; sprinkle with brown sugar. Return to oven for an additional 5 minutes, or until marshmallows are golden. Serves 8 to 12.

Serve a sweet potato casserole in orange cups...so pretty on a dinner buffet! Cut large oranges in half and scoop out the orange pulp with a grapefruit spoon. Shells can even be prepared a day ahead and refrigerated. Heap the sweet potato mixture in the shells, place in a baking pan and bake as directed.

Barley & Sweet Corn Bake

Julie Francis
Cape Girardeau, MO

This hearty, colorful casserole goes well with pork, chicken or fish.
For convenience, it can be made ahead and refrigerated.

3 cloves garlic, minced
1 c. onion, chopped
2/3 c. carrots, peeled
   and chopped
1 T. oil
3 c. chicken broth

1 c. pearled barley, uncooked
Optional: 1/4 t. salt
1/8 t. pepper
2 c. frozen corn, thawed
1/2 c. fresh parsley, chopped

In a skillet over medium heat, sauté garlic, onion and carrots in
oil until tender. Transfer to a greased 2-quart casserole dish; add
broth, barley, salt if desired and pepper. Mix well. Cover and bake
at 350 degrees for one hour. Stir in corn and parsley. Cover and
bake an additional 10 to 15 minutes, or until barley is tender and
corn is heated through. Makes 10 to 12 servings.

Make quick & easy "snowballs" to tuck into the Christmas
tree or nestle in an evergreen centerpiece. Simply cut
snowy white quilt batting into narrow strips and roll it
into balls. Add a pinch of frosty silver glitter, if you like.

Mom's Oyster Dressing

LeeAnn Edwards
Billings, MO

For several years Mom made this dish for our family Thanksgiving and Christmas dinners. My dad and brothers still request it every year so now I make it. It doesn't taste quite the same as Mom's, but it's close!

14-3/4 oz. can creamed corn
8-oz. can smoked oysters,
   drained
1/2 c. evaporated milk

1/2 c. butter, softened
1 sleeve saltine crackers,
   crumbled

In a lightly greased 12"x8" baking pan, mix all ingredients in order given. Add more crackers if a thicker consistency is desired. Bake, uncovered, at 350 degrees for 35 to 40 minutes. Serves 4 to 6.

Be sure to share your family's stories behind the special foods that are a tradition at every holiday dinner... Grandmother's green bean casserole, Aunt Jessie's famous walnut cake, Mom's secret seasoning for the roast beef. There may even be stories to tell about the vintage tablecloth or the whimsical salt & pepper shakers!

Simply Elegant Steak & Rice

Kelly Marcum
Rock Falls, IL

*From my Aunt Jean, a most wonderful hostess and cook. On one of
our first trips out after having our first child, she had this dish
simmering on the stove when we walked in the door.*

1-1/2 lbs. boneless beef round
   steak, sliced into 1-inch
   strips
1-1/2 t. oil
2 onions, sliced into rings
10-3/4 oz. can cream of
   mushroom soup

1/2 c. dry sherry or beef broth
4-oz. can sliced mushrooms,
   drained and liquid reserved
1-1/2 t. garlic salt
4 c. cooked rice

In a large skillet over medium-high heat, brown beef in oil. Add
onions; sauté until crisp-tender. Blend soup, sherry or broth,
reserved mushroom liquid and garlic salt; pour over beef mixture.
Add mushrooms. Reduce heat to low; cover and simmer for about
one hour, until beef is tender. Serve over cooked rice. If desired,
dish may be prepared in the oven. Transfer skillet mixture to a
greased 2-quart casserole; cover and bake at 350 degrees for
45 to 60 minutes. Serves 6.

Get in the holiday spirit by
trimming a tabletop tree! Look
around the house for items like
sparkly clip earrings or tiny toys
and dolls to use as ornaments...even
clip figures from Christmas cards or
make a tiny paper chain. Such fun!

Holiday Broccoli Casserole

Lori Havens
Lisle, IL

As a girl growing up in Michigan, I enjoyed visiting my Aunt Johanna, Uncle Hal and all my cousins on Christmas Eve. Aunt Johanna served this yummy casserole on many special occasions, and I was happy to receive the recipe. When I married, I brought this dish to my new family's holiday table...and it has been on their menus ever since!

10-oz. pkg. frozen chopped
   broccoli, cooked and drained
1 egg, beaten
1/4 c. milk
1/4 c. mayonnaise

1/2 c. shredded Cheddar cheese
10-3/4 oz. can cream of
   mushroom soup
1/2 c. zweiback toast, crumbled
2 T. butter, melted

Place broccoli in a greased shallow 8"x8" baking pan. Stir together egg, milk, mayonnaise, cheese and soup; pour over broccoli. Combine toast crumbs and butter; sprinkle evenly over casserole. Bake, uncovered, at 350 degrees for 45 minutes. Serves 6.

The best gift busy parents could receive...an offer to babysit for an afternoon or an evening. While they're out holiday shopping, entertain the kids with a simple activity like baking cookies or making sweet handprint cards for Mom & Dad. Your gesture is sure to be appreciated.

Lemon-Chive Potatoes

Stefanie St. Pierre
North Chatham, MA

These are our favorite potatoes...they're really delicious!

1 T. olive oil
1 lb. redskin potatoes, cubed
salt and pepper to taste

1/2 c. water
3 chives, thinly sliced
1 t. lemon juice

In a large pot, heat oil over medium-high heat. Add potatoes; sprinkle with salt and pepper. Cook, tossing occasionally, until golden, about 10 to 15 minutes, adding a little more oil if needed. Add water; stir and cover. Cook until potatoes are tender and liquid has evaporated, about 5 minutes. Transfer to a serving bowl; toss potatoes with chives and lemon juice. Makes 4 servings.

While you're adding the finishing touches to a big holiday meal, set out a wooden bowl of whole walnuts or pecans and a nutcracker for guests. It'll double as a party activity and a light snack...before you know it, dinner is served!

Farmhouse Christmas Dinner

Nut-Crusted Baked Chicken

Micah Tannehill
Springfield, MO

Everyone loves this supper...it's really good for any occasion!
Just add rice pilaf and steamed, buttered broccoli for
an elegant meal that's oh-so easy to prepare.

6-oz. pkg. cornbread stuffing
   mix
1/4 c. almonds
1/4 c. walnuts
1/4 c. French fried onions
1/2 t. pepper

1 egg, beaten
3 T. warm water
10-3/4 oz. can cream of
   mushroom soup
4 boneless, skinless chicken
   breasts

Combine stuffing mix, almonds, walnuts, onions and pepper in a
blender. Pulse mixture to the texture of cornmeal; place in a shallow
bowl. In a separate shallow bowl, whisk egg and water together.
Add soup to egg mixture and beat until well blended. Dip chicken
breasts into egg mixture and then into stuffing mixture until well
coated. Place in a greased 13"x9" baking pan. Bake, uncovered,
at 400 degrees until chicken juices run clear when pierced, about
45 minutes. Serves 4.

Share the spirit of the season with the whole
neighborhood...go caroling! Make up little booklets
with words of popular carols ahead of time, if you like.
Don't worry about singing off-key...you'll be terrific!

Cheesy Eggplant Casserole

Allison Antony
Washington, VA

A yummy meatless main! Garnish with a toss of chopped parsley.

1 eggplant, peeled and sliced
   1/4-inch thick
1 c. onion, sliced
1 clove garlic, crushed
2 T. oil
2 tomatoes, sliced 1/2-inch
   thick

2 t. sugar
1 t. dried basil
1 t. dried oregano
salt to taste
8-oz. pkg shredded mozzarella
   cheese
1/2 c. grated Parmesan cheese

Bring a large saucepan of salted water to a boil over medium-high heat. Add eggplant slices. Simmer 5 to 10 minutes until just tender, but not mushy. Drain well and set aside. In the same saucepan over medium heat, sauté onion and garlic in oil; drain. Layer eggplant and tomato slices alternately in a greased 12"x8" baking pan, overlapping slightly. Sprinkle with sugar and seasonings. Top with onion mixture; sprinkle evenly with cheeses. Bake, uncovered, at 375 degrees for 30 to 40 minutes, until hot and bubbly. Serves 6.

It seems there's always more than enough food on Christmas Day...why not set an extra place and invite a neighbor or co-worker who might otherwise spend the day alone. Can't think of anybody? Just check with a neighborhood church or senior center.

OLD-FASHIONED
Desserts

Cider Apple Pie

Barbara Cooper
Orion, IL

*Nothing says "Welcome home!" like a homemade apple pie
fresh from the oven. With Cheddar cheese baked right into
the crust, this one is even more delicious than usual.*

6 c. Jonagold apples, cored,
   peeled and sliced
1 c. apple cider
2/3 c. sugar
2 T. cornstarch

1/2 t. cinnamon
3 T. cold water, divided
1 T. butter
1 egg yolk

Combine apples, cider and sugar in a saucepan over medium-high
heat. Bring to a boil; reduce heat and simmer 5 minutes. In a small
bowl, dissolve cornstarch and cinnamon in 2 tablespoons water.
Stir into apple mixture; cook and stir until mixture comes to a boil.
Remove from heat; stir in butter. Arrange one Cheddar Crust in a
9" pie plate; spoon in filling. Add top crust and crimp edges together.
Cut slits in crust to allow steam to escape. Beat egg yolk and
remaining water with a fork; brush over crust. Cover edge of crust
with a strip of aluminum foil to prevent overbrowning. Bake at
400 degrees for 35 to 40 minutes, until filling is bubbly and crust
is golden. Cool to room temperature before cutting. Serves 8.

Cheddar Crust:

2 c. all-purpose flour, sifted
2/3 c. shortening
1 c. finely shredded Cheddar
   cheese

5 to 6 T. water

Cut together flour and shortening until crumbly; stir in cheese. Add
water, one tablespoon at a time, just until dough sticks together.
Form dough into 2 balls. Roll each into a 9-inch round.

A multitude of small delights constitutes happiness.

–Charles Baudelaire

126

Mini Pecan Tartlets

Brittany Crawford
Friendship, TN

My kids love these yummy little individual pies...they're easy to make too! After the tartlets have cooled, you can dress them up with a spoonful of whipped cream and a pecan half on top.

1/2 c. cream cheese, softened
1/2 c. plus 1 t. butter, softened
   and divided
1 c. all-purpose flour
3/4 c. brown sugar, packed

1 egg, beaten
1 t. vanilla extract
1/8 t. salt
1 c. chopped pecans

Blend cream cheese and 1/2 cup butter; mix in flour. Cover and chill while making filling. In a separate bowl, mix together remaining ingredients. Form chilled dough into 24 small balls. Press each ball into the bottom and up the sides of a greased mini muffin cup to form a crust. Spoon in pecan filling. Bake at 350 degrees for 15 to 20 minutes, until golden. Makes 2 dozen.

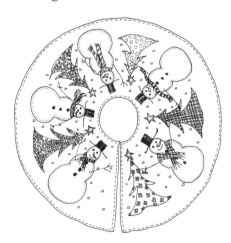

In need of a tree skirt? A jolly vintage Christmas tablecloth with its brightly colored images of Santas, elves or carolers is easily wrapped around the tree for a bit of old-fashioned holiday fun.

Pumpkin Ice Cream Pie

Vickie
Gooseberry Patch

This scrumptious pie is a convenient make-ahead recipe...the pie can be prepared and tucked into the freezer up to a month ahead of time. The yummy Butterscotch Sauce can be made ahead and rewarmed.

15-oz. can pumpkin
2/3 c. brown sugar, packed
1 t. ground ginger
1 t. cinnamon
3/4 t. nutmeg
1/8 t. ground cloves

3 pts. vanilla ice cream, divided
9-inch graham cracker crust,
   frozen
Optional: whipping cream,
   whipped

Stir pumpkin, brown sugar and spices together in a saucepan over low heat. Cook and stir until sugar dissolves and mixture thickens. Refrigerate until cool, about 2 hours. Soften 2 pints of ice cream and blend with pumpkin mixture; spread evenly into crust. Cover; freeze at least 2 hours. Soften remaining pint of ice cream and spread over pie; return to freezer. At serving time, let pie stand for a few minutes at room temperature before slicing. Serve topped with Butterscotch Sauce and whipped cream, if desired. Serves 6 to 8.

Butterscotch Sauce:

1/4 c. butter
1 c. brown sugar, packed

1 c. whipping cream

In a small saucepan over low heat, melt butter. Stir in brown sugar until dissolved. Add cream and bring to a boil, stirring continuously. Remove from heat; cool. Refrigerate in a covered container.

A vintage canning jar filled with a favorite homemade sauce makes a thoughtful hostess gift. Tie on a topper of colorful holiday fabric with ribbon along with instructions for enjoying your gift.

Old-Fashioned Desserts

Red Velvet Christmas Cake

Peggy Frazier
Indianapolis, IN

This is a really old family recipe, so old my copy calls for a stick of "oleo." Ha! I use this family recipe throughout the year for several holidays. For Valentine's Day, I bake it in heart-shaped pans, and it is a beautiful 4th of July cake too. Of course it's a must at Christmastime. When my now-grown daughter, Julie, was young, I helped her make this cake for her father to take to work for a pitch-in fundraiser. She won 1st prize and still has the blue ribbon to prove she can bake. I hope everyone who tries this cake makes it a family tradition also!

2-1/2 c. all-purpose flour
1-1/2 c. sugar
1 t. salt
1 t. baking cocoa
1 c. buttermilk
1-1/2 c. oil

2 eggs, beaten
1 t. vanilla extract
1-oz. bottle red food coloring
1 t. white vinegar
1 t. baking soda

In a large bowl, sift flour, sugar, salt and cocoa together. Add buttermilk, oil, eggs and vanilla; mix well. Stir in food coloring. Mix vinegar and baking soda together in a cup. Add to batter; mix only until well blended. Pour into 3 greased and floured 9" round cake pans. Bake at 325 degrees for 30 to 35 minutes, until a toothpick inserted in center tests clean. Cool slightly; turn out of pans onto a wire rack and cool completely. Assemble and frost cake with Cream Cheese Frosting. Serves 10 to 12.

Cream Cheese Frosting:

8-oz. pkg. cream cheese,
  softened
1/2 c. margarine
1 t. vanilla extract

6 c. powdered sugar
Optional: 1/3 c. chopped pecans

Blend cream cheese, margarine and vanilla. Stir in powdered sugar until well mixed. Add nuts, if desired.

Cherry Brownie Cobbler

Amy Hunt
Traphill, NC

I found this recipe while looking for something new to make for a Sunday dessert. Your friends & family will love this cobbler...it's delicious! The chocolate and cherries really complement each other.

20-oz. pkg. brownie mix
1/2 c. water
1/2 c. oil
1 egg, beaten

21-oz. can cherry pie filling
1/4 c. butter, softened
8-1/2 oz. pkg. yellow cake mix
Garnish: vanilla ice cream

Prepare brownie mix according to packaging directions, using water, oil and egg. Spread batter into a 13"x9" baking pan sprayed with non-stick vegetable spray. Bake at 350 degrees for 15 minutes; remove from oven. Spread pie filling over brownie layer; set aside. Cut butter into dry cake mix until crumbly. Sprinkle mixture over pie filling. Return to oven and continue to bake an additional 45 to 50 minutes, until filling is set. Cool completely; cut into squares. Serve topped with scoops of ice cream. Serves 10 to 12.

Aprons are a great project for a beginning seamstress...who wouldn't love a gift of a sweet or spunky new apron? There are lots of simple patterns and charming fabrics available. If you're making an apron for a child, use the scraps to make a tiny apron for her favorite dolly too.

Sweet Cinnamon Pie

Janet McRoberts
Lexington, KY

This is an old-fashioned family recipe we have enjoyed for years. You'll hardly believe such a tasty dessert can be made with such simple ingredients!

1/2 T. all-purpose flour
3 T. sugar
2 T. cinnamon
2 T. butter, softened

3 eggs, beaten
2 c. milk
9-inch pie crust

Mix flour, sugar, cinnamon and butter together. Stir in eggs and milk; pour into unbaked pie crust. Bake at 350 degrees for 45 to 50 minutes, until set. Cool before slicing. Serves 8.

Fill small fabric bags with pine needles, tiny pine cones, dried orange peel, whole cloves and cinnamon sticks. Tie them closed with ribbon and hang on the kitchen's door knobs. Each time the doors are opened, the sachets will release a spicy holiday scent.

Honey Bun Cake

Jill Gordon
Marceline, MO

My Aunt Julie shared this recipe with me...now it's a must at every family get-together.

18-1/2 oz. pkg. yellow
   cake mix
3/4 c. oil
4 eggs, beaten
8-oz. container sour cream

1 c. brown sugar, packed
1 T. cinnamon
2 c. powdered sugar
1 T. vanilla extract
1/4 c. milk

Stir dry cake mix, oil, eggs and sour cream together until well mixed. Pour batter into a greased 13"x9" baking pan; set aside. Mix together brown sugar and cinnamon. Sprinkle mixture over batter; swirl into batter with a table knife. Bake at 325 degrees for 40 minutes. Whisk together remaining ingredients; pour onto cake while still warm. Serves 12.

Nothing says "country-fresh flavor" like dollops of whipped cream on a warm homebaked dessert. In a chilled mixing bowl, with chilled beaters, beat a cup of whipping cream on high speed until soft peaks form. Stir in 2 teaspoons sugar and 2 teaspoons vanilla extract...now, wasn't that easy?

Cream Cheese Pumpkin Squares

Pamela Elkin
Asheville, NC

This recipe is so quick & easy to make that it's one of my favorites to share during the holidays. Be sure to have extra copies of the recipe on hand...everyone will be asking you for it!

8-oz. pkg. cream cheese,
  softened
14-oz. can sweetened
  condensed milk
3 eggs, divided

15-oz. can pumpkin
3 t. pumpkin pie spice, divided
16-oz. pkg. pound cake mix
2 T. butter, melted
1 c. chopped pecans

Beat cream cheese until fluffy; add condensed milk and beat well. Add 2 beaten eggs, pumpkin and 2 teaspoons spice. Mix well and set aside. Combine dry cake mix, butter and remaining egg and spice. Mix with an electric mixer on low speed until crumbly. Press mixture into the bottom of a greased 13"x9" baking pan to form a crust. Pour cream cheese mixture over crust; sprinkle with nuts. Bake at 350 degrees for 30 to 35 minutes, until set. Chill; cut into squares. Keep refrigerated. Makes 2 to 3 dozen.

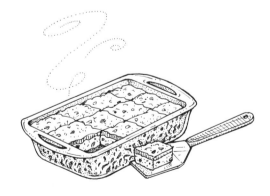

Brush craft glue onto bare twigs and sprinkle with frosty silver or white glitter. Arrange the twigs in a vase for a pretty buffet decoration in a jiffy.

Mocha Pudding Cake

Lanita Anderson
Chesapeake, VA

This delicious recipe was given to me by a fellow chaplain's wife. Even guests who don't usually care for the flavor of coffee love this cake!

1 c. all-purpose flour
1 c. sugar, divided
6 T. baking cocoa, divided
1-1/2 t. baking powder
1/4 t. salt
1/2 c. milk
3 T. oil

1 t. vanilla extract
1/2 c. mini semi-sweet
  chocolate chips
1 c. brewed strong coffee
Garnish: vanilla ice cream or
  whipped topping

Combine flour, 2/3 cup sugar, 4 tablespoons cocoa, baking powder and salt in a large bowl. In a separate bowl, stir together milk, oil and vanilla. Add to dry ingredients, stirring just until blended. Spread batter evenly into a lightly greased 8"x8" baking pan. Combine chocolate chips with remaining sugar and cocoa; sprinkle evenly over batter. Bring coffee to a boil; pour evenly over batter. Do not stir. Bake at 350 degrees for 25 to 30 minutes, or until cake springs back when lightly pressed in center. Garnish as desired. Serves 8 to 10.

Dust powdered sugar through a doily for a pretty
yet simple cake decoration...check craft stores
for holiday stencils too!

Cheery Cran-Pear Cobbler

Gloria Robertson
Midland, TX

*This yummy, fruit-filled cobbler is wonderful for brunch
as well as dessert.*

2 15-1/4 oz. cans sliced pears
  in syrup
1 c. sweetened dried
  cranberries
1/4 c. instant tapioca,
  uncooked
1 c. applesauce
1/4 t. nutmeg

2 t. cinnamon, divided
1 c. sugar
2 12-oz. tubes refrigerated
  buttermilk biscuits
1/2 c. butter, melted
Garnish: vanilla ice cream or
  whipped topping

Pour pears with syrup into a greased 8"x8" baking pan. Sprinkle
with cranberries and tapioca; set aside. Combine applesauce with
nutmeg and one teaspoon cinnamon. Mix well and spoon over fruit.
Bake at 450 degrees for 10 to 20 minutes, until hot and bubbly.
Remove from oven; reduce oven temperature to 400 degrees.
In a pie plate or shallow dish, combine sugar and remaining
cinnamon; mix well. Separate biscuits. Dip each biscuit in butter,
then in cinnamon-sugar to coat both sides. Arrange biscuits over
fruit. Bake at 400 degrees for 15 to 20 minutes, or until biscuits are
golden. Cool about 20 minutes. Serve warm; garnish as desired.
Makes 8 servings.

Make a family recipe scrapbook...invite everyone to
share tried & true family favorites like Mom's sugar
cookies and Aunt Betty's chocolate pecan pie.
A gift idea everyone will love!

Caramel-Glazed Apple Cake

Brenda Smith
Delaware, OH

This made-from-scratch cake with its luscious glaze is irresistible! It's easy to tote to holiday get-togethers or potlucks in its baking pan too.

1-1/2 c. butter, softened
1 c. sugar
1 c. brown sugar, packed
3 eggs
3 c. all-purpose flour
1 t. baking soda
1/2 t. salt

1 T. cinnamon
1 t. nutmeg
5 Granny Smith apples, cored, peeled and diced
1-1/4 c. chopped pecans
2-1/4 t. vanilla extract

In a large bowl with an electric mixer on medium-high, beat butter and sugars until light and fluffy. Beat in eggs, one at a time. In a separate bowl, combine flour, baking soda, salt and spices. With a wooden spoon, gradually add flour mixture to butter mixture to form a very thick batter. Stir in remaining ingredients. Pour batter into a greased and floured 13"x9" baking pan. Bake at 325 degrees for 50 to 60 minutes, until a toothpick inserted in center comes out clean. Cool cake in pan on a wire rack for at least 10 minutes. With a fork, poke holes all over surface of cake. Pour warm Caramel Glaze over cake. Serve warm or cooled. Serves 16.

Caramel Glaze:

1/4 c. butter
1/4 c. sugar
1/4 c. brown sugar, packed

1/8 t. salt
1/2 c. whipping cream

In a saucepan over medium-low heat, melt butter. Add sugars and salt. Cook, stirring frequently, for 2 minutes. Stir in cream and bring to a boil. Cook, stirring constantly, for 2 minutes.

Creamy Eggnog Pie

Dale Duncan
Waterloo, IA

Every Christmas we can hardly wait until cartons of holiday eggnog appear in the grocer's dairy department...that means it's time to make this rich, festive pie!

1 T. unflavored gelatin
1/4 c. cold water
1/3 c. sugar
2 T. cornstarch
1/4 t. salt
2 c. eggnog

1 t. vanilla extract
1 t. rum extract
2 c. whipped cream
9-inch graham cracker crust
Garnish: additional whipped
   cream, nutmeg

Soften gelatin in cold water; set aside. In a saucepan over medium-low heat, combine sugar, cornstarch and salt. Stir in eggnog until smooth. Bring to a boil; cook and stir for 2 minutes, or until thickened. Stir in gelatin mixture until dissolved. Remove from heat; cool to room temperature. Stir in extracts. Fold in whipped cream. Pour into pie crust. Cover and chill for 4 hours. Serve topped with a dollop of whipped cream and a sprinkle of nutmeg. Makes 6 to 8 servings.

Need a way to keep the kids busy while they're waiting for Santa's big day? Show them how to cut snowflakes from folded paper, then let them scatter a blizzard of snowflakes around the house...on the tree, down the banister, even taped to gift-wrapped packages. Old-fashioned fun!

Fudgy Pudding Cake

Wilda Bartenschlag
Lewisville, OH

A super-easy way to turn a cake mix into something really special!

1 c. brown sugar, packed
1/2 c. baking cocoa
2 c. water
2 c. mini marshmallows
18-1/2 oz. pkg. chocolate
   cake mix

Optional: 1 c. pecan, peanut
   or walnut pieces
Garnish: whipped topping or
   vanilla ice cream

Mix brown sugar, cocoa, water and marshmallows in a greased 13"x9" baking pan; set aside. Prepare cake mix as directed on package; spoon batter over mixture in pan. Top with nuts, if desired. Bake at 350 degrees for 45 to 50 minutes, until a toothpick inserted in center tests clean. Serve warm or cooled, garnished as desired. Serves 16.

Bake a favorite holiday cake like gingerbread or red velvet cake in holiday-patterned paper cupcake liners. The cupcakes will look so inviting arranged on a tiered cake stand.

Peppermint Bark Brownies

Angie Biggin
Lyons, IL

These brownies are welcome at any holiday occasion! Everyone loves chocolate and peppermint at Christmas.

20-oz. pkg. fudge brownie mix
12-oz. pkg. white chocolate
  chips

2 t. margarine
1-1/2 c. candy canes, crushed

Prepare and bake brownie mix according to package directions, using a greased 13"x9" baking pan. After baking, set aside and cool completely in pan, about one to 2 hours. In a saucepan over very low heat, melt chocolate chips and margarine, stirring constantly with a rubber spatula. Spread chocolate mixture over brownies; sprinkle with crushed candy. Let stand for about 30 minutes, until frosting is hardened. Cut into squares. Makes 2 dozen.

Scraps of vintage fabric add a sweet touch to handmade ornaments and stockings or tied around a stack of recipe cards as a gift.

Molasses Chiffon Pie

Eleanor Dionne
Beverly, MA

*This sweet old-fashioned pie was a special dessert that my mother
always baked for holiday and Sunday dinners.*

1 T. unflavored gelatin
1/4 c. cold water
3 eggs
3/4 c. light molasses
2 T. orange juice
1/2 t. cinnamon

1/8 t. salt
1 c. whipping cream
9-inch shortbread crumb crust
Optional: shaved chocolate
   curls

Soften gelatin in cold water; set aside. Beat eggs until light; add
molasses and mix well. Pour mixture into the top of a double boiler.
Cook over hot water, stirring constantly, until thick. Stir in gelatin
mixture, orange juice, cinnamon and salt. Chill until slightly
thickened. With an electric mixer on high speed, whip cream stiffly;
fold into molasses mixture. Pour into crust and chill until firm.
Sprinkle shaved chocolate curls over pie, if desired. Serves 6.

For a yummy, fun dessert that's ready in a jiffy, spoon warm
chocolate pudding into mugs. Top with whipped cream
and chocolate sprinkles, hot cocoa style.

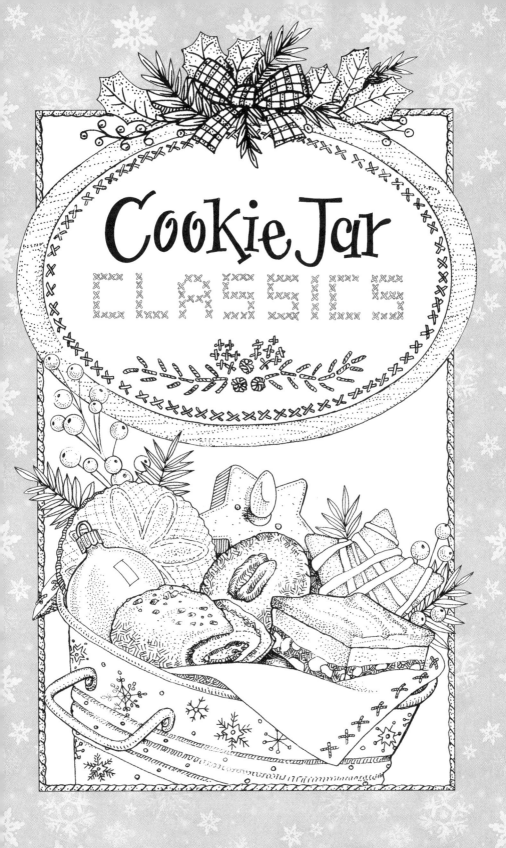

Cookie Jar
CLASSICS

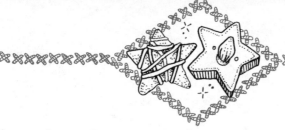

Chocolate Spice Cookies

Sandy Ellis
Caledonia, OH

These cookies were the favorite of my mother, Charlotte Beal. We always baked special cookies for Christmas...some of my best memories are of baking with Mom. When the first batch of these cookies came out of the oven, we would have our coffee ready and always "tested" them to make sure they tasted as good as they smelled!

4 c. all-purpose flour
1/2 c. baking cocoa
4 t. allspice
1/2 t. ground cloves
2 t. cinnamon
1/4 t. salt

1-1/2 c. sugar
1 c. plus 2 T. shortening,
   melted and slightly cooled
1-1/2 c. milk
1/2 t. vanilla extract
1-1/2 c. chopped walnuts

Mix all dry ingredients in a large bowl; set aside. In a separate bowl, combine shortening, milk and vanilla. Add dry ingredients to shortening mixture. Stir in walnuts. Drop by tablespoonfuls onto greased or parchment paper-lined baking sheets. Bake at 350 degrees for 10 minutes. Makes 5 dozen.

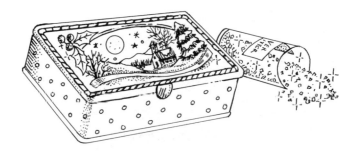

Pretty Christmas tins are a bargain at tag sales...don't pass them up! With a quick scrub and a fresh lining of parchment paper, they're as good as new. When the holidays roll around, you'll have plenty of containers to fill with homemade goodies for gift-giving.

Maple Pecan Drops

Kathy Larson
Worthington, MO

These cookies are absolutely scrumptious! Press them together in pairs with maple-flavored frosting for a yummy sandwich cookie.

2 c. all-purpose flour	1-1/2 t. maple extract
1/2 c. sugar	1/4 t. salt
1/4 c. brown sugar, packed	1 egg, beaten
1 c. butter, softened	16-oz. pkg. pecan halves

Combine flour, sugars, butter, extract and salt in a large bowl. With an electric mixer on low speed, beat until blended, occasionally scraping bowl with a spatula. Add egg; blend well. Increase speed to medium; beat until dough is light and fluffy. Roll dough into balls by rounded teaspoonfuls; place about one inch apart on ungreased baking sheets. Gently press a pecan half into the top of each ball. Bake at 350 degrees for 12 to 14 minutes, until lightly golden. Cool cookies slightly on baking sheet; remove to wire racks to cool completely. Store in a tightly covered container for up to 2 weeks. Makes 5 dozen.

Have a cookies & punch party! Bake and freeze cookies in advance, as time allows. The day before, mix up a punch to refrigerate and remove cookies from the freezer to thaw. At party time, pour the punch into a punch bowl, arrange cookies on trays, tie on a frilly holiday apron and greet your guests.

Santa's Whiskers

Kendra Walker
Hamilton, OH

*In years gone by, I always made dozens of Christmas cookies
to share with family & friends. This recipe is one of my son's
favorites...he just loves maraschino cherries!*

1 c. butter, softened
1 c. sugar
2 T. milk
1 t. vanilla extract
2-1/2 c. all-purpose flour

3/4 c. maraschino cherries,
   drained and finely chopped
1/2 c. pecans, finely chopped
3/4 c. sweetened flaked
   coconut

Blend together butter and sugar; mix in milk and vanilla. Stir in flour,
cherries and pecans. Form dough into 2 logs, each 8 inches long.
Roll logs in coconut to coat dough. Wrap in wax paper or plastic
wrap; chill dough for several hours to overnight. Slice 1/4-inch thick;
place on ungreased baking sheets. Bake at 375 degrees until edges
are golden, about 12 minutes. Makes 5 dozen.

Bake a chocolatey version of a favorite sugar cookie.
Choose a recipe that calls for at least 2-1/4 cups
all-purpose flour, and replace 1/4 cup of the flour with
1/4 cup baking cocoa. Add the other usual ingredients,
then melt a one-ounce square of semi-sweet baking
chocolate and stir it in. Roll out dough,
cut out cookies and bake...yum!

Chocolate Oat Chews

*Tawnia Hultink
Ontario, Canada*

This is an absolute favorite bar of so many people, I get asked for it all the time. My Tante Gertje shared it with us...her baking is the best!

3/4 c. butter, softened
1 c. brown sugar, packed
1-1/2 c. quick-cooking oats,
   uncooked
1-1/4 c. all-purpose flour

1/2 t. baking soda
1/2 t. salt
4 c. mini marshmallows
1 c. semi-sweet chocolate chips

Blend together butter and brown sugar in a large bowl. In a separate bowl, combine oats, flour, baking soda and salt; add to butter mixture. Stir well; set aside 1-1/2 cups of mixture for topping. Press remaining mixture into the bottom of a greased 13"x9" baking pan. Sprinkle marshmallows, chocolate chips and reserved oat mixture on top; press lightly. Bake at 375 degrees for 20 minutes, or until golden. Cool; cut into bars. Makes 2 dozen.

A red enamelware pail is just right for
displaying newly arrived Christmas cards...
tuck in a sprig of pine-scented greenery.

Brownie Thins

Jo Ann
Gooseberry Patch

*If you like your brownies crisp, you'll love these
thin, chocolatey cookies.*

6 T. butter, sliced
2 1-oz. sqs. unsweetened
   baking chocolate, chopped
1/2 c. sugar
1 egg, beaten

3 T. plus 1 t. all-purpose flour
1/4 t. vanilla extract
1/4 t. almond extract
1/8 t. salt
1/4 c. chopped walnuts

Place butter and chocolate in a microwave-safe bowl. Microwave on medium-high setting until almost melted, about one minute. Whisk until smooth. Add sugar and egg; whisk again until smooth. Stir in flour, extracts and salt; let stand for 10 minutes. Drop batter by rounded teaspoonfuls onto greased baking sheets. Cover baking sheets with plastic wrap sprayed lightly with non-stick vegetable spray. Press each mound of batter into a 2-1/2 inch circle. Peel off plastic wrap. Sprinkle nuts over cookies. Place oven rack in lower third of oven. Bake cookies at 350 degrees, one sheet at a time, for about 7 minutes, until slightly darker at edges and firm in centers. Cool on baking sheet 2 minutes. Transfer to a wire rack; cool completely. Makes 2 dozen.

The next time you pick up the Christmas cards in your mailbox, why not slip in a sweet treat for the letter carrier? You could even tuck in a gift card for a cup of hot coffee at a nearby coffee shop... how thoughtful!

Spicy Pepper Nuts

Kathy Harris
Valley Center, KS

I love the licorice flavor of these tiny, tasty cookies! I make them for our church's craft show...many people are so delighted to find Pepper Nuts that they buy 3 or 4 bags. They are crisp and ready to eat as soon as they cool. I prefer these over the soft kind.

1 c. margarine, softened
1-1/2 c. sugar
1/2 t. anise oil
1 egg, beaten
2 T. light corn syrup

3 c. all-purpose flour
1 t. baking soda
1 t. ground cloves
1 t. ground ginger
1 t. cinnamon

In a large bowl, blend together margarine, sugar and oil. Add remaining ingredients; stir well until flour is no longer visible. Cover and refrigerate for one hour, until firm. Roll dough into 1/2-inch thick logs; slice cookies 1/4-inch thick. Place on ungreased baking sheets. Cookies can be placed very close to each other since they don't spread very much. Bake at 350 degrees for 10 to 12 minutes, just until lightly golden. Makes about 16 dozen.

Tuck spiced teabags into holiday letters and invite far-away friends to sip a cup of tea while catching up on the latest news from you.

Lemon-Macadamia Cookies

Brenda Melancon
Gonzales, LA

*One of my daughters, Lisa, loves macadamia nuts and I love lemon,
so I combined our favorite flavors to create these tasty cookies.*

3/4 c. butter, softened
1 c. sugar
1 c. brown sugar, packed
2 eggs
3.4-oz. pkg. instant lemon
   pudding mix
2-1/4 c. all-purpose flour

1 t. baking soda
1/4 t. salt
2 t. lemon zest
1 t. lemon extract
1 c. macadamia nuts, coarsely
   chopped
1/2 c. toffee baking bits

Combine butter and sugars in a large bowl. Beat with an electric
mixer on medium speed until light and fluffy. Add eggs; beat until
combined. In a separate bowl, combine dry pudding mix, flour,
baking soda, salt and zest. Slowly add to butter mixture. Add
extract; beat until combined. Stir in nuts and toffee bits. Drop by
rounded tablespoonfuls onto ungreased baking sheets, 2 inches
apart. Bake at 350 degrees for 10 to 12 minutes, until lightly golden
around edges. Cool cookies on baking sheets for 2 minutes. Remove
to wire racks to cool completely. Makes 4 dozen.

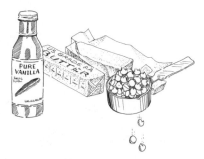

By mid-autumn, you'll find grocery specials on many
items needed for holiday baking...chocolate chips,
vanilla extract, candied fruits, brown sugar and flour.
Stock your pantry and save!

"Buttermilk" Cinnamon Bars

Tina Dillon
Parma, OH

This has been my go-to cookie recipe for years. My kitchen cupboard is stocked with the basic ingredients, and I always have pecans in the freezer! There's no actual buttermilk...the vinegar-and-milk mixture is the secret substitute!

2 c. all-purpose flour
1-1/4 c. sugar
1/4 c. brown sugar, packed
1/2 c. butter, softened
1/2 c. chopped pecans
1 t. baking soda

1 t. cinnamon
1 c. milk
1 T. white vinegar
1 t. vanilla extract
1 egg, beaten

Mix together flour, sugars and butter until crumbly. Press 2 cups mixture into the bottom of a ungreased 13"x9" baking pan. Add remaining ingredients to remaining crumb mixture; stir well. Spread over crumb crust. Bake at 350 degrees for 20 to 25 minutes, or until a toothpick tests clean. Let cool completely before spreading with Almond Frosting. Cut into bars after frosting sets. Makes 2 dozen.

Almond Frosting:

2 c. powdered sugar
1/4 t. almond extract

3 to 4 T. milk, divided

Combine powdered sugar and almond extract. Stir in milk to desired frosting consistency.

Gifts of time and love are surely the basic
ingredients of a truly merry Christmas.

–Peg Bracken

Butter Pecan Cookies

Lisa Johnson
Hallsville, TX

When I was a kid, this was one of my parents' favorite cookies...either homemade or store-bought. These cookies will keep about two weeks, if you can stay out of the cookie jar!

18-oz. pkg. butter pecan cake
   mix
5-1/4 oz. pkg. instant vanilla
   pudding mix

1 egg, beaten
1 c. oil
1 c. chopped pecans

Mix together all ingredients. Drop by tablespoonfuls onto greased baking sheets. Bake at 350 degrees for 8 to 10 minutes. Makes about 3 dozen.

Start a new family tradition. December 26 is Boxing Day, when gifts would be given to those less fortunate. It's a good day to gather up toys, clothing and housewares that are no longer needed but still good, and deliver them to local charities.

Holly Jolly Cookies

Mary Kelly
Jefferson City, MO

My daughter, Erin, and I get together on a Saturday to bake about fifteen different kinds of cookies all in one day. It's one of my favorite Christmas traditions...our family calls it "The Great Cookie Extravaganza"! We've been doing this for at least ten years. Then we fill plates, wrap them with a bow and deliver them to the neighbors. Everyone looks forward to it so much!

6 c. corn flake cereal
1/2 c. margarine
10-oz. pkg. marshmallows
1 T. green food coloring

1 t. vanilla extract
9-oz. pkg. red cinnamon
  candies

Put cereal in a large bowl and set aside. In a saucepan over very low heat, melt margarine and marshmallows; mix well. Stir in food coloring and vanilla. Pour marshmallow mixture over cereal; mix until well coated. Drop by teaspoonfuls onto wax paper. Top each cookie with 3 to 4 cinnamon candies and let cool. Makes about 3 dozen.

When you go out on Christmas Eve to attend church services or see the Christmas lights, drop off a plate of homemade cookies at your local fire or police station...it's sure to be much appreciated.

Soft Chocolate Chip Cookies

Marsha Porter
Marysville, OH

Who doesn't love chocolate chip cookies? These are the best!

16-oz. pkg. butter, softened
1/2 c. sugar
1-1/2 c. brown sugar, packed
2 3.4-oz. pkgs. instant vanilla
   pudding mix
2 t. vanilla extract
4 eggs, beaten
4-1/2 c. all-purpose flour

1 c. long-cooking oats,
   uncooked
2 t. baking soda
12-oz. pkg. semi-sweet
   chocolate chips
Optional: 1 c. chopped pecans
   or walnuts

In a very large bowl, blend butter and sugars together. Add pudding mix and vanilla; beat until smooth and creamy. Stir in eggs. In a separate bowl, combine flour, oats and baking soda. Gradually beat flour mixture into butter mixture. Stir in chocolate chips and nuts, if using. Drop by teaspoonfuls onto greased baking sheets. Bake at 350 degrees for 8 to 10 minutes. Makes 6 dozen.

Snow fun! Fill several squirt bottles with warm water and
a few drops of food coloring, then send the kids out to
"paint" the snow...they'll love it!

Cranberry Oat Cookies

Diana Decker
Kerhonkson, NY

I've been baking my mom's oatmeal-raisin cookie recipe ever since I was a young girl. One day, I decided to create something different for the holiday season so I tried using cranberries instead of raisins. Everyone liked them so much that now I make them often! They're a nice change and very festive-looking for the holidays.

1-1/4 c. margarine, softened
3/4 c. dark brown sugar, packed
1/2 c. sugar
1 egg, beaten
1 t. vanilla extract
1-1/2 c. all-purpose flour
1 t. baking soda

1/2 t. salt
1 t. cinnamon
1/4 t. nutmeg
3 c. long-cooking oats, uncooked
1 c. sweetened dried cranberries
1 c. white chocolate chips

Blend margarine, sugars, egg and vanilla in a very large bowl. Add remaining ingredients and mix well. Using rounded teaspoonfuls of dough, roll into 1-1/4 inch balls. Place on ungreased baking sheets; flatten cookies slightly. Bake at 375 degrees, 8 to 9 minutes for chewy cookies, 10 to 11 minutes for crisp cookies. Cool on baking sheets 2 to 3 minutes before removing to wire racks. Makes about 4 to 4-1/2 dozen.

A fun family outing! Tuck some cookies for snacking in your pocket and go to a zoo to see some real live reindeer.

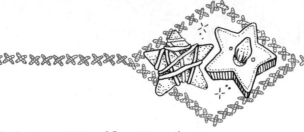

Mom's Waffle Cookies

Amanda Carlisle
Palm Coast, FL

Every year at Christmas, my mom would mix the dough for these cookies, then my sister and I would bake them on the waffle iron. It was so much fun, we didn't realize that we were doing all of the work! Now it just isn't Christmas without these yummy treats on the cookie tray.

16-oz. pkg. butter, melted and
   cooled
8 eggs, beaten
2 c. sugar
1 c. brown sugar, packed

1 t. vanilla extract
1 t. baking soda
1/4 t. salt
8-1/2 to 9 c. all-purpose flour

In a very large bowl, mix butter with eggs, sugars and vanilla. Stir in baking soda, salt and enough flour to make a stiff dough. Roll into walnut-size balls. Place in a preheated greased waffle iron and bake about 2 minutes, or until golden. Makes 8 dozen.

Chocolate Buttercream Frosting

Tina Wright
Atlanta, GA

Yum...this homemade chocolate frosting really makes your cookies extra special.

1/4 c. butter, softened
2 c. powdered sugar
3 T. baking cocoa

1 t. vanilla extract
2 to 3 T. milk

Mix together all ingredients, adding milk a little at a time to make a spreadable consistency. Use immediately. Makes about 2 cups.

Jan Hagels

Eileen Bennett
Jenison, MI

I have been making these traditional Dutch cookies since the early 1960s. Because they are easy to make and easy to tote, I would often make them when I was asked to bring a dessert to a church supper. "Simply delicious!" is the remark I often heard.

1 c. butter, softened
1 c. sugar
1 egg, separated
1 t. vanilla extract

2 c. all-purpose flour
1/2 c. sliced almonds or
    chopped pecans

Blend butter and sugar; stir in egg yolk, vanilla and flour. Press dough thinly onto an ungreased 15"x10" jelly-roll pan. Whisk egg white; brush over dough. Sprinkle with nuts and press nuts down into dough slightly. Bake at 350 degrees for 25 minutes, or until lightly golden. Immediately cut into traditional diamond shapes, or into bars or squares. Makes 2 to 3 dozen.

Handed-down cookie recipes offer a taste of tradition that just can't be beat. If you weren't lucky enough to receive recipes from Mom or Grandma, why not check the cookbook section of your neighborhood library? It's possible you will rediscover the very recipe you remember loving as a kid.

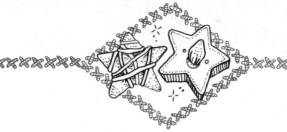

Walnut Rugalach

Karen Sampson
Waymart, PA

The most popular Christmas cookies on my holiday trays! I have made them for weddings, showers and parties...they always sell out at our church bake sale too. Taste them and you'll find out why!

1-1/2 c. butter, divided
8-oz. pkg. cream cheese,
   softened
2 c. all-purpose flour

1-1/2 c. sugar
1-1/2 T. cinnamon
6 T. walnuts, finely chopped
   and divided

Place one cup softened butter and cream cheese in a large bowl. Beat with an electric mixer on low speed until smooth. Beat in flour. Divide dough into 4 portions; form each into a disk. Wrap in plastic wrap; chill until firm, about one hour. Combine sugar and cinnamon; set aside. On a floured surface, roll one disk into a 10-inch circle. Brush with one tablespoon melted butter; sprinkle evenly with 2-1/2 tablespoons cinnamon-sugar and one tablespoon nuts. With a pizza cutter, cut circle into 12 wedges. Roll up wedges from wide end to point. Place on ungreased baking sheets, 2 inches apart. Bend into crescent shapes. Repeat with remaining dough. Bake at 350 degrees for 28 minutes, or until golden. Let cool slightly. While still warm, lightly brush with remaining butter; sprinkle with remaining cinnamon-sugar. Remove to wire racks to cool. Makes 4 dozen.

Turn Christmas treats into sweetly wrapped treasures...
use pretty papers, handcrafted tags and cheery
red & white ribbons.

Melt-in-Your-Mouth Cookies

Sheila Murray
Tehachapi, CA

My dad says these taste just like the sugar cookies his mother used to make for him when he was little. I like to use a glass tumbler with a fancy bottom to flatten the cookies...so pretty!

1 c. sugar
1 c. powdered sugar
1 c. butter, softened
1 c. oil
2 eggs, beaten
1 t. vanilla extract

4-1/3 c. all-purpose flour
1 t. cream of tartar
1 t. baking soda
1/2 t. salt
Garnish: white or colored sugar

Blend sugars along with butter, oil, eggs and vanilla. In a separate bowl, combine remaining ingredients except garnish. Stir well and add to wet mixture, mixing well. Cover dough and chill until firm, about 2 hours. Roll teaspoonfuls of dough into balls and place on ungreased baking sheets. Grease the bottom of a small glass; dip in desired sugar and flatten each cookie. Bake at 350 degrees for 8 to 10 minutes, until lightly golden. Makes about 3 dozen.

Favorite Cookie Frosting

Tonya Sheppard
Galveston, TX

Here's a tasty twist...instead of vanilla extract, add one tablespoon of finely grated orange or lemon zest.

1/2 c. butter, softened
16-oz. pkg. powdered sugar
3 T. half-and-half

2 t. vanilla extract
Optional: several drops food
  coloring

With an electric mixer on low speed, beat butter until very smooth. Add powdered sugar, half-and-half and vanilla; beat until very smooth. Tint with food coloring, if desired. Makes 2 cups.

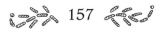

Piña Colada Cookies

Peggy Market
Elida, OH

Christmas wouldn't be complete without my dad making these zingy cookies. He would get such a thrill out of making them and giving them in beautiful Christmas tins for the holidays! It's one of my special memories of Dad in the kitchen.

1 c. sugar	2 eggs, beaten
1/2 c. butter	2-3/4 c. all-purpose flour
1 t. vanilla extract	1 t. baking powder

Blend sugar, butter and vanilla together; add eggs and mix well. Slowly stir in flour and baking powder. Form into 3 balls; cover and refrigerate for one hour. Sprinkle flour on a pastry cloth. Roll out one ball at a time to 1/4-inch thick. Cut out cookies with desired cookie cutters and place on lightly greased baking sheets. Bake at 350 degrees for 10 to 12 minutes, watching to avoid overbaking. Frost cookies when cooled. Makes 2 dozen.

Pina Colada Frosting:

3 c. powdered sugar	3 to 4 t. liquid piña colada mix
1 t. shortening	

Mix powdered sugar with shortening and piña colada mix to desired consistency.

Cheery holiday potholders with pockets can be found at any grocery. Slip several wrapped cookies (and the recipe!) into the pocket for handy keep-on-hand gifts.

Christmas Meringues

Peggy Cummings
Cibolo, TX

These simple cookies conceal a treasure inside...a bite of chocolate and peppermint! The ice pulse on my blender makes quick work of crushing the candies.

2 egg whites
1/8 t. salt
1/8 t. cream of tartar
3/4 c. sugar
1/2 t. vanilla extract

3 T. peppermint candies, crushed
2 c. mini semi-sweet chocolate chips

Place egg whites in a small bowl. Beat with an electric mixer on high speed until foamy. Add salt and cream of tartar; continue beating. Add sugar, one tablespoon at a time, beating well after each addition until stiff peaks form. Gently fold in remaining ingredients with a rubber spatula. Drop by teaspoonfuls, 1-1/2 inches apart, on baking sheets sprayed with non-stick vegetable spray. Bake at 250 degrees for 40 minutes. Remove to wire racks to cool completely. Store in airtight tins. Makes 3 dozen.

Turn meringue cookies into cute snowman faces...press on mini chocolate chips and red cinnamon candies with a bit of frosting to make eyes, noses and mouths.

Annabel's Pumpkin Cookies

Lecia Stevenson
Timberville, VA

This recipe was given to me by my sister, Annabel...these cookies are wonderful! The combination of pumpkin and chocolate chips makes them delicious and healthy.

1 c. canned pumpkin	1 t. cinnamon
1 c. sugar	1/2 t. salt
1/2 c. oil or applesauce	1 t. baking soda
1 egg, beaten	1 t. milk
2 c. all-purpose flour	1 t. vanilla extract
2 t. baking powder	1 c. semi-sweet chocolate chips

Combine pumpkin, sugar, oil or applesauce and egg. In a separate bowl, stir together flour, baking powder, cinnamon and salt. Add pumpkin mixture to flour mixture; stir well. Dissolve baking soda in milk; add to dough and mix well. Stir in remaining ingredients. Drop by teaspoonfuls onto lightly greased baking sheets. Bake at 350 degrees for 10 to 12 minutes. Makes 2-1/2 dozen.

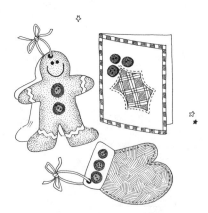

Gingerbread people gift tags...so cute! Trace around cookie cutters onto brown kraft paper, cut them out and decorate with mini white rick rack "frosting." Punch a hole at top and tie onto gifts with a bit of yarn.

So-Yummy Chocolate Bars

JoAnna Haughey
Berwyn, PA

Friends with a sweet tooth will absolutely love these bars!

1 c. butter, softened
1/2 c. sugar
1/8 t. salt
2 c. all-purpose flour
14-oz. can sweetened
   condensed milk

1 c. semi-sweet or milk
   chocolate chips
1/2 c. chopped walnuts
1 t. vanilla extract

In a large bowl, beat butter with an electric mixer on medium speed for 30 seconds. Add sugar and salt; continue beating until blended. Reduce mixer speed to low; beat in flour until combined. Press 2/3 of mixture into the bottom of an ungreased 13"x9" baking pan; set aside. Combine condensed milk and chocolate in a saucepan. Stir over low heat until chocolate melts and mixture is smooth. Remove from heat; stir in remaining ingredients. Spread hot mixture over layer in pan. Dot with remaining flour mixture. Bake at 350 degrees for 35 minutes, or until golden. Cool completely; cut into squares. Makes 2 dozen.

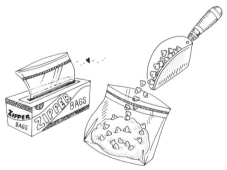

Drizzle melted chocolate over cookies in a jiffy! Fill a plastic zipping bag with chocolate chips and microwave briefly, until melted. Snip off a tiny corner and drizzle away...afterwards, just toss away the bag.

Orange Drop Cookies

Edye VanHouten
Fort Wayne, IN

Everyone loves these easy-to-make cookies! With their fresh orange flavor, they're like a taste of summer in chilly weather.

2/3 c. oil
3/4 c. sugar
1 egg, beaten
2 c. all-purpose flour
1/3 t. baking powder

1/2 t. baking soda
1/2 t. salt
1/2 c. orange juice
2 T. orange zest

Mix oil, sugar and egg together; set aside. In a separate bowl, sift dry ingredients together; add to oil mixture. Stir in remaining ingredients. Drop by rounded teaspoonfuls onto greased baking sheets, about 2 inches apart. Bake at 400 degrees for 8 to 10 minutes. Frost cookies with Orange Frosting while still warm. Makes 2-1/2 to 3 dozen.

Orange Frosting:

2 c. powdered sugar
1 T. oil

1 T. orange zest
1 to 2 t. orange juice

Mix powdered sugar, oil and orange zest. Carefully stir in orange juice to desired smoothness.

Super-speedy snickerdoodles! Roll a tube of refrigerated sugar cookie dough into one-inch balls. Coat them in a mixture of 3 tablespoons sugar and one teaspoon cinnamon. Bake on ungreased baking sheets, 10 to 13 minutes at 350 degrees. Cool on wire racks. Yummy!

Grandma's Gingerbread Men

Vicki Fender
Westport, WA

My husband's grandmother shared this recipe with me in 1978.
I still follow her advice, "Don't roll too thin or bake too long!"
The spices fill my kitchen with warmth and love.

1/2 c. shortening
1/2 c. sugar
1 egg, beaten
1/2 c. light molasses
2 c. all-purpose flour
1 t. baking powder

1/2 t. baking soda
1/2 t. salt
1-1/2 t. cinnamon
1 t. ground ginger
1/2 t. ground cloves
Optional: frosting, raisins

In a large bowl, beat shortening until creamy. Gradually add sugar, beating until light and fluffy. Add egg and molasses; beat well and set aside. In a separate bowl, combine flour, baking powder, baking soda, salt and spices. Add to shortening mixture, mixing well. Roll out dough to 1/8-inch thickness on a well-floured board. Cut out cookies with a 5-inch gingerbread man cutter; place on ungreased baking sheets. Bake at 375 degrees for 9 minutes. Cool for one minute on baking sheets; remove to a wire rack to cool completely. Decorate cookies with frosting and raisins, if desired. Makes one dozen.

Host a gingerbread house party for the neighborhood kids! A trip to the grocery store will yield lots of fun decorations for a yummy gingerbread house...candy-coated chocolates, cinnamon candies, peppermints, cereal shapes and mini pretzels. Just use your imagination!

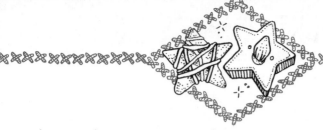

Almond Butter Cookies

Tammy Kobza
Ireton, IA

These cookies look beautiful, taste scrumptious and are simple to make. I usually take them to our school's annual Christmas bake sale and they go fast. There are no eggs in this recipe.

1 c. butter	2 c. all-purpose flour
3/4 c. sugar	1/2 t. baking powder
1 t. almond extract	1/4 t. salt

Place butter in a microwave-safe bowl and heat about 10 seconds, until very soft but not melted. Stir together butter, sugar and extract. Add dry ingredients; mix well. If dough seems too dry, add another tablespoon or so of butter. Form into one-inch balls; place on ungreased baking sheets. Flatten to 1/4-inch thickness with the bottom of a glass jar. Bake at 400 degrees for 6 to 8 minutes. Let cool. Drizzle Chocolate Glaze over cookies; let stand until glaze sets. Makes 5-1/2 to 6 dozen.

Chocolate Glaze:

1/2 c. semi-sweet chocolate chips	2 t. shortening

In a small saucepan, stir ingredients over very low heat until melted and smooth.

Be a cookie elf! Wrap up plates of cookies to leave secretly at the neighbors' doorsteps...don't get caught!

Holiday Strawberries

Lavonda Payne
Boaz, AL

These old-fashioned confections look so pretty on a candy or cookie tray. If desired, insert a sliver of green candied cherry for the stem.

3 3-oz. pkgs. strawberry
  gelatin mix
14-oz. can sweetened
  condensed milk

2 c. pecans, finely chopped
2 c. sweetened flaked coconut
Garnish: red and green colored
  sugar

Beat gelatin mix and condensed milk together until smooth. Add pecans and coconut; mix just until combined. Dampen hands with a little water; form mixture into 1-1/2 inch strawberry shapes. Roll sides of strawberries in red sugar; dip tops in green sugar. Place in an airtight container with wax paper between layers; keep refrigerated for up to 2 weeks. Makes about 4 dozen.

The children were nestled all snug in their beds,
While visions of sugarplums danced in their heads.

–Clement Clark Moore

Cherry-Walnut Fudge

Tammy Thomas
Quecreek, PA

*I was making peanut butter fudge for my friends at work when
I remembered that I had maraschino cherries in the refrigerator.
So I gave this recipe a try...I'm glad I did!*

3 c. sugar
12-oz. can evaporated milk
10-oz. jar maraschino cherries,
   drained, chopped and liquid
   reserved

1 t. vanilla extract
1/4 c. plus 1 t. margarine
1 c. white chocolate chips
1 c. chopped walnuts

In a large heavy saucepan over medium-high heat, combine sugar,
evaporated milk and 1/4 cup reserved cherry liquid. Bring to a
boil. Stirring constantly, cook until mixture reaches soft-ball stage,
234 to 243 degrees on a candy thermometer. Remove from heat.
Add remaining ingredients. Stir with a wooden spoon until
chocolate chips melt and mixture starts to thicken. Pour into a
buttered 15"x10" jelly-roll pan. Let cool before cutting into squares.
Makes 3 dozen.

For friends with a sweet tooth, spoon warm homemade
fudge into individual red or green silicone muffin cups and
top with candy sprinkles. Wrap up each cup of fudge in
plastic wrap and add a bow...delightful!

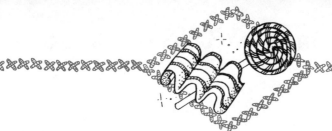

Coconut-Almond Candies

Marcia Reps
Utica, MN

Family & friends will be impressed with these yummy, multi-layered candies...but they're not really that hard to make.

2 c. sweetened flaked coconut,
   chopped
3 T. sweetened condensed milk
3 T. powdered sugar
2 t. butter, softened
12-oz. pkg. semi-sweet
   chocolate chips

8-oz. pkg. white melting
   chocolate, chopped
1 T. shortening
2-1/4 oz. pkg. whole almonds

In a large bowl, beat coconut, condensed milk, sugar and butter together until blended; set aside. Place chocolate chips, melting chocolate and shortening in a microwave-safe bowl. Microwave on high setting for one to 2 minutes; stir until melted and smooth. Spoon about 1/2 teaspoon of chocolate mixture into each of 42 paper-lined mini muffin cups. Form coconut mixture into balls by 1/2 teaspoonfuls; gently press into chocolate. Top each with an almond. Spoon one teaspoon of remaining chocolate mixture over each. Let stand until set. Store in an airtight container. Makes 3-1/2 dozen.

Fill mini take-out containers with homemade candies
and tie curling ribbons onto the handles. Pile them
in a wicker basket as welcome favors for holiday visitors.

Homemade Sweets to Share

Microwave Pecan Brittle

Beckie Apple
Grannis, AR

My grandmother always made pecan brittle for the holidays. She used to tell me, "It's so easy anyone can do it." But I feared that mine just would not turn out like hers, so I never tried it. After she had passed away, I was going through some recipes she had given to me and discovered the recipe again. I was determined to make it and I did. It turned out just like hers...just like she said, it's so easy anyone can do it!

3 t. butter, softened and
   divided
1 t. vanilla extract
1 t. baking soda

3/4 c. pecans, finely chopped
1 c. sugar
1/2 c. light corn syrup

Line a baking sheet with aluminum foil. Butter foil with one teaspoon butter; set aside. Place remaining butter, vanilla, baking soda and pecans in a bowl; set aside. In a microwave-safe 2-quart glass bowl, mix sugar and corn syrup; stir well. Microwave on high for 5 minutes. With a wooden spoon, stir 3 to 4 times. Microwave again for 3 to 4 minutes, until mixture begins to turn a light toffee color. Remove from microwave very carefully, as mixture is extremely hot. Stir 3 times; immediately add remaining ingredients. Stir 3 to 4 times. Mixture will be thick. Quickly pour onto the buttered baking sheet. Allow to cool completely for 30 to 40 minutes. Break into pieces and store in an airtight container. Makes 10 to 12 servings.

Simple shipping tags can become gift tags in a snap...just glue on a vintage sticker, buttons or a family photo!

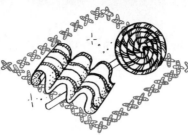

Nutty Mixed-Up Popcorn

Carol Johnson
Yakima, WA

My sister-in-law included some of this white chocolate popcorn treat in a Christmas gift basket. It is now a family favorite. When we have our annual bowling fun day, I am expected to bring this...knowing that certain people look forward to it, once a year, makes it special!

4 3-oz. pkgs. microwave
  popcorn, popped
16-oz. can cashew halves and
  pieces

9-oz. pkg. corn chips
20-oz. pkg. white melting
  chocolate, chopped

Pour popped popcorn into a large roasting pan that been lightly sprayed with non-stick vegetable spray. Add cashews and corn chips to popcorn; toss to mix and set aside. Place melting chocolate in a microwave-safe bowl. Microwave on high setting for one minute; stir and microwave an additional minute, until melted. Pour over popcorn mixture. Mix with a spoon or buttered hands, coating well. Let stand for 10 minutes; cover with aluminum foil or divide into 4 large plastic zipping bags. May be stored at room temperature up to a week. Makes about 16 cups.

A new white paper paint bucket from the hardware store
is easily turned into a super gift for a movie lover. Decorate
the bucket with glued-on movie cut-outs, then fill it
with packages of microwave popcorn and other goodies.
Tuck in a couple of movies on DVD for a gift that
will long be remembered!

Homemade Sweets to Share

Cream Cheese Fudge

Christine Schnaufer
Geneseo, IL

Each Christmas we enjoy this easy treat and remember my husband's mother. She used to make this fudge for him over sixty years ago...it is still one of his fond memories.

1/2 c. butter, softened
12-oz. pkg. milk chocolate
   chips
1/4 t. salt
2 8-oz. pkgs. cream cheese,
   room temperature

2 16-oz. pkgs. powdered sugar
1 t. vanilla extract
2 c. walnuts, finely chopped

Combine butter, chocolate chips and salt in a microwave-safe large bowl. Microwave on low setting for 3 to 4 minutes; stir. Add cream cheese and microwave one additional minute. Beat well with an electric mixer on medium speed. Add powdered sugar and vanilla; beat well. Stir in nuts and pour into a buttered 13"x9" baking pan. Chill until firm; cut into squares. Makes about 3 dozen.

Top homemade chocolate fudge with crushed peppermint candies or a drizzle of white chocolate for a decorative finish in a jiffy.

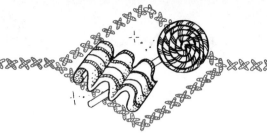

Reindeer Chow

JoAnna Haughey
Berwyn, PA

This recipe makes enough crunchy snack mix to give as gifts for all your favorite people...teachers, bus drivers, scout leaders, coaches. They're sure to love it!

3 c. bite-size crispy rice cereal
3 c. bite-size crispy corn cereal
3 c. doughnut-shaped oat
  cereal
3 c. pretzel sticks

16-oz. pkg. red and green candy-coated chocolates
3 12-oz. pkgs. white chocolate chips, melted

In a very large heat-proof bowl or roaster, toss together all ingredients except chocolate chips; set aside. Melt chocolate chips in a double boiler over hot water; stir until smooth. Pour melted chocolate over cereal mixture; stir until well coated. Spread mixture on wax paper-lined baking sheets or trays to set. Break up into bite-size pieces; store in airtight containers. Makes about 14 cups.

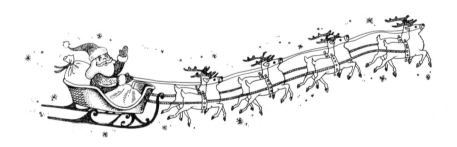

Make a whimsical reindeer canister to fill with sweet or savory snack mix. Cover an empty coffee can using red paper and craft glue. Cut an oval of brown felt for the reindeer's face and small felt triangles for the ears. Add pipe cleaner antlers, a red pompom nose and two googly eyes...how cute!

Peanutty Chocolate Clusters

Sara Moulder
LaGrange, OH

*Made in a slow cooker, this is an unbelievably easy candy recipe...
and it's scrumptious! I love to make it at Christmastime
to share with family & friends.*

16-oz. pkg. salted peanuts
16-oz. pkg. unsalted peanuts
12-oz. pkg. semi-sweet
   chocolate chips
2 16-oz. pkgs. white melting
   chocolate, chopped

4 1-oz. sqs. sweet baking
   chocolate
Optional: 1 c. raisins

Spray a large slow cooker with non-stick vegetable spray. Add all ingredients except raisins. Cover and cook on low setting for 3 hours. Stir until well mixed. Stir in raisins, if desired. Drop by teaspoonfuls onto wax paper-lined baking sheets. Cool; store in covered containers. Makes about 9 dozen.

Don't toss out your Christmas cards after the holidays have ended! Cut them into gift tags and tuck them away with the ornaments, so you'll be sure to find them next Christmas.

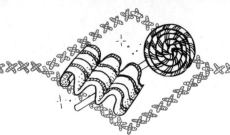

Tasty Toffee Candy

Cheryl Walker
Syracuse, NY

My mom handed down this candy recipe to me and it has remained special to our family for years, especially around the holiday season. It makes a delightful gift!

36 saltine crackers
1 c. butter, sliced
1 c. dark brown sugar, packed

2 c. semi-sweet chocolate chips
Optional: 1/4 c. chopped pecans
or nuts of your choice

Line a baking sheet with parchment paper or aluminum foil. Spray with non-stick vegetable spray. Arrange saltine crackers on baking sheet with sides touching; set aside. In a heavy saucepan over medium heat, slowly boil butter and brown sugar together for 4 minutes, stirring often and being careful not to burn. Pour hot mixture over crackers. Immediately bake at 375 degrees for 5 minutes. Remove from oven; sprinkle with chocolate chips and nuts, if using. Refrigerate overnight. Break into pieces. Store in a covered container. Serves 8.

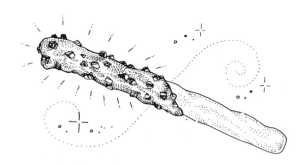

A sweet & salty treat that's a snap to make! Simply dip pretzel rods in melted chocolate. Drizzle with white chocolate if you like, then roll in candy sprinkles. Pack the pretzel rods in tall vintage canning jars or wrap them individually in plastic wrap and tie with a ribbon.

Homemade Caramels

Andrea Heyart
Aubrey, TX

My grandma has made these caramels every Christmas for as long as I can remember. One year she hadn't gotten around to making caramels by Christmas Eve. Everyone complained so much that she went to the kitchen at 9 o'clock at night and whipped them up. That year we realized how important food traditions really are to our family...thanks, Grandma!

2 c. sugar
2 c. light corn syrup
2 c. butter

12-oz. can evaporated milk
1 t. vanilla extract

Place sugar and corn syrup in a heavy saucepan. Bring to a boil over medium-high heat; do not burn. Boil mixture, stirring, for about 15 to 20 minutes until it reaches the thread stage, or 230 to 233 degrees on a candy thermometer. Add butter; once melted, add evaporated milk. Keep boiling an additional 15 to 20 minutes, until it reaches the firm-ball stage, 244 to 249 degrees on a candy thermometer. Remove from heat; add vanilla. Pour into a greased 15"x10" jelly-roll pan. When cool, cut into 1-1/2 to 2-inch squares. Wrap in small squares of wax paper. Makes about 1-1/2 dozen.

Make a nutty dessert topping to spoon over ice cream or sliced pound cake...yum! Mix a cup of toasted walnuts with a cup of maple syrup and place in a jar. Pecans and honey are scrumptious too. The topping may be stored at room temperature up to two weeks.

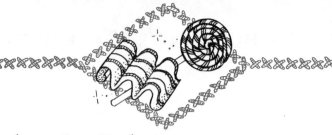

Chocolate-Oat Fudge

Diane Owens
Maysville, KY

This is my brother's favorite treat...he looks forward to me making it for him every Christmas.

1/2 c. milk
2 c. sugar
1/2 c. butter
1/4 c. baking cocoa

1 T. vanilla extract
1/2 c. creamy peanut butter
2 c. quick-cooking oats, uncooked

In a saucepan over medium heat, mix together milk, sugar, butter and cocoa. Bring to a boil; boil for 5 minutes, stirring frequently. Stir in remaining ingredients. Pour into a greased 11"x8" glass baking pan. Let cool before cutting into squares. Makes 16 pieces.

For someone far away, a care package of sweets is a terrific surprise! Along with homemade candies, tuck in a phone card and some family photos...so thoughtful!

Peanut Butter Crunch Candy

Paula Stow
Chino, CA

*Always a crowd-pleaser and so easy to make. It's a fairly soft,
rich candy, so you don't need a big piece to feel satisfied.*

16-oz. pkg. white melting
   chocolate, chopped
1/2 c. crunchy peanut butter

2 c. crispy rice cereal
2 c. mini marshmallows

Line a 13"x9" baking pan with parchment paper, allowing some
paper to hang over long edges of pan; set aside. Place chocolate in
a microwave-safe bowl. Microwave on high for 2 minutes; stir.
If not all the chocolate is melted, microwave for another 30 to
45 seconds. Stir in peanut butter; mix thoroughly. Fold in cereal and
marshmallows, keeping marshmallows as whole as possible. Pour
mixture into parchment paper-lined baking pan. Cool for 30 minutes
in refrigerator, or about 1-1/2 hours at room temperature. Remove
candy, lifting out by the parchment paper. Peel off paper and cut
candy into one-inch squares. Store in an airtight container. Makes
about 8 dozen.

If you cross-stitch, it's easy to whip up a gift for a friend.
On a 5-inch fabric square, cross-stitch a fun message like
"Treats for You." Glue batting to the top of a canning jar
lid, top with stitched square, then glue it inside the
jar ring. Let it dry and fill your jar with goodies!

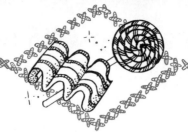

Holiday Hard Candy

Phyllis Peters
Three Rivers, MI

Some thirty-five years ago, a lady in our church used to make this candy each Christmas, giving a jar of it to each Sunday school teacher. I asked her for the recipe. Packed in a clear glass jar, it's very colorful and will keep for quite some time, so it's a great gift.

2 c. sugar
3/4 c. water
2/3 c. light corn syrup

1 t. flavoring oil
6 to 10 drops food coloring
Garnish: powdered sugar

In a heavy saucepan over medium-high heat, combine sugar, water and corn syrup. Cook, stirring occasionally, until mixture reaches the hard-crack stage, or 290 to 310 degrees on a candy thermometer. Remove from heat. Mixture will be very hot, so handle carefully. Stir in flavoring and a few drops of food coloring. Pour into a greased 13"x9" baking pan. When cool, break or cut into pieces. Toss with powdered sugar to coat. Store in an airtight jar or container. Makes about 2 pounds.

Some candy recipes call for flavoring oils, also called candy oils. These are made especially for candy making, come in tiny bottles and are three to four times stronger than extracts. Look for flavoring oils in lots of yummy flavors at a grocery store or drugstore.

Snowy Trail Mix

Heather Plasterer
Colorado Springs, CO

*So easy and so yummy! I have given it in little cellophane bags
tied with a cute ribbon for gifts...everybody loves them.*

3 c. mini pretzel sticks
1-1/2 c. bite-size corn & rice
   cereal squares
3/4 c. pecan halves
1/2 c. sweetened dried
   cranberries

1/2 c. cashew halves
1 c. red and green
   candy-coated chocolates
12-oz. pkg. white melting
   chocolate, chopped

In a large microwave-safe bowl, mix all ingredients except
white chocolate; set aside. Place white chocolate in a separate
microwave-safe bowl. Microwave chocolate on high for one to
2 minutes; stir until smooth. Slowly pour melted chocolate over
pretzel mixture, gently stirring until evenly covered with chocolate.
Scoop out onto wax paper. Let cool 20 minutes; break into bite-size
clusters. Makes 10 cups.

Pick up a pack of white paper lunch sacks and wrap up
a lot of sweet gifts in a hurry. Simply fill the bags
with goodies, fold over the tops twice and add a
brightly colored sticker...done!

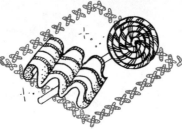

Sunflower Seed Brittle

Angie Venable
Ostrander, OH

Since I'm from Kansas, the Sunflower State, of course I had to try this deliciously different recipe for homemade brittle...I'm glad I did!

1 T. butter
1 c. dry-roasted sunflower
   kernels

1/4 t. salt
1 c. sugar

Melt butter in a small saucepan over low heat. Add sunflower kernels and salt; mix well and cover to keep warm. Carefully melt sugar in a heavy skillet over medium heat, stirring constantly. Sugar will be extremely hot. When sugar is golden, quickly stir in warm sunflower kernel mixture. Pour out onto a buttered baking sheet. Using a wooden spoon, quickly spread into a 10-inch by 10-inch square. Let cool until firm; break into bite-size pieces. Store in an airtight container. Makes about 3/4 pound.

Keep little hands busy making button wreaths! Choose large, flat plastic buttons from Grandma's button box or pick up a supply at a craft store. Simply thread buttons onto wire, then twist the ends to form a circle. Tie on a fluffy bow and they're ready to hang on the tree!

Gathering
WITH
FRIENDS

Festive Cranberry Salsa

Vickie
Gooseberry Patch

Serve this fresh-tasting salsa with white corn tortilla chips
or spoon it over baked chicken...scrumptious!

1/2 c. cranberry juice cocktail
1-1/2 c. diced tomatoes,
   drained
1 c. cranberries, finely chopped
1/2 c. crushed pineapple,
   drained
1/2 c. green onions, thinly
   sliced

1/4 c. avocado, peeled, pitted
   and diced
1/4 c. jalapeño pepper, finely
   chopped
2 T. lemon juice
2 cloves garlic, pressed

Pour cranberry juice into a medium saucepan; bring to a boil over
medium-high heat. Boil for about 5 minutes, until juice is reduced
to one tablespoon. Add remaining ingredients. Return to a boil;
stir until well mixed. Cover and chill before serving. Serves 8.

Make holiday entertaining extra easy with an
all-appetizers party! Set up tables in different areas so
guests can mingle as they enjoy yummy spreads and finger
foods. Your get-together is sure to be a festive success.

Chinese Chicken Spread

Lisa Colombo
Appleton, WI

This easy recipe is a hit with our bunco night crowd! Look for the rice crackers in the Asian food section of your grocery store.

8-oz. pkg. cream cheese,
  softened
1-3/4 c. cooked chicken breast,
  shredded
3 T. green onions, sliced
1/2 c. carrots, peeled and
  grated

1/2 t. ground ginger
3 T. soy sauce
1 clove garlic, minced
1/2 c. slivered almonds
Garnish: sweet-and-sour sauce
teriyaki-flavored rice crackers

Spread softened cream cheese onto a platter. Mix all remaining ingredients except sauce and crackers in a bowl; spread over top of cream cheese layer. Drizzle with sauce. To serve, arrange crackers around edge of platter. Serves 8.

Give a grapevine wreath a brand-new look...it's simple!
Coat it with white spray paint. While the paint is still wet,
dust the wreath with fine white glitter for icy sparkle.

Mississippi Fun Dip

Pat Cornett
Smithfield, VA

When this appetizer was served at my friend's 50th birthday party, it was voted the best by all the guests...even the kids! A long, thick loaf of bread works best.

1 loaf Italian bread
2 8-oz. pkgs. cream cheese, softened
1 c. sour cream
2 c. shredded Cheddar cheese

2 c. cooked ham, diced
4-oz. can diced green chiles, drained
1/4 c. green onions, diced
scoop-type corn chips

Slice off top of loaf lengthwise and scoop out the bread inside, reserving bread for dipping. Combine remaining ingredients except corn chips. Blend well and spoon mixture into loaf. Replace top of loaf; wrap in aluminum foil. Bake at 400 degrees for one hour and 15 minutes. Unwrap carefully and remove top of loaf. Serve with corn chips and reserved bread pieces. Serves 8 to 10.

Share the cheer! Invite party guests to bring along
a can of food. Gather all the cans in a big wicker basket
and drop off at a local food pantry.

Glazed Chicken Wings

Phyl Broich-Wessling
Garner, IA

These juicy wings have become a year 'round favorite.

6 T. orange juice
5 T. honey
2 T. white wine or chicken
   broth
2 T. orange zest
1 T. lemon juice
1 t. ground ginger

1 t. coriander seed, crushed
1 t. pepper
1/2 t. cinnamon
12 chicken wing drummies
Garnish: thin strips orange
   zest, fresh orange sections,
   fresh mint leaves

In a large bowl, mix together all ingredients except chicken wings and garnish. Add chicken wings to bowl; cover and refrigerate for at least 4 hours to overnight. Line a small roasting pan with a double layer of aluminum foil. Transfer wings and glaze mixture to pan, arranging wings so the thickest pieces are along the outer edges of the pan. Bake for 50 to 60 minutes at 375 degrees, basting frequently with glaze, until chicken juices run clear. If glaze is still very liquid at the end of the baking time, pour it off into a small saucepan and boil rapidly until reduced and thickened. Spoon glaze over wings; continue baking for an additional 10 minutes. Wings may be served hot or cold, garnished as desired. Serves 4.

Make a special CD music mix of all-time Christmas favorites, or set your CD player to shuffle for a variety of very merry music...it's sure to get the party going!

Vintage Party Mix

Marian Buckley
Fontana, CA

When my sister and I were growing up in the 1950s, my mom always served this party mix at the parties she and Dad hosted. Sis and I would creep downstairs to peek at the guests in their elegant clothing. A handful of this crunchy mix brings it all back to me!

6 T. butter, sliced
4 t. Worcestershire sauce
3/8 t. garlic powder
3/8 t. seasoned salt
2 c. bite-size crispy wheat
   cereal squares

2 c. bite-size crispy rice cereal
   squares
2 c. bite-size crispy corn cereal
   squares
3/4 c. salted mixed nuts

Place butter in a deep 13"x9" baking pan or roaster; heat in a 250-degree oven until melted. Stir in Worcestershire sauce, garlic powder and seasoned salt. Add cereal squares and nuts; toss to mix well. Bake, uncovered, at 250 degrees for 45 minutes, stirring every 15 minutes. Spread on paper towels to cool. Store in an airtight container. Makes about 7 cups.

Everyone loves a Christmas stocking full of goodies!
For a grown-up version of this fun tradition, decorate mini
paper gift bags to hang on the mantel instead of stockings.

Patricia's Super Nachos

Patricia Addison
Cave Junction, OR

These nachos are served at our home whenever we watch
football bowl games on television. Make a double batch
to feed a whole tailgating crowd!

1 lb. ground beef
1 yellow onion, chopped
1 t. salt
1/2 t. pepper
2 16-oz. cans refried beans
4-oz. can diced green chiles
hot pepper sauce to taste
3 c. shredded Cheddar cheese

3/4 c. taco sauce
1 c. guacamole
8-oz. container sour cream
1/4 c. green onions, chopped
2-1/4 oz. can chopped black
   olives, drained
tortilla chips

Brown ground beef and onion in a skillet over medium heat. Drain;
add salt and pepper and set aside. Spread beans in the bottom of an
ungreased 15"x10" jelly-roll pan. Top with ground beef mixture,
chiles, hot pepper sauce and cheese; drizzle taco sauce over the top.
Bake, uncovered, at 400 degrees for 25 minutes, until heated
through and cheese is melted. Remove from oven; top with
remaining ingredients except tortilla chips. Serve warm with tortilla
chips. Serves 12.

I wish we could put up some of the Christmas spirit
in jars and open a jar of it every month.

–Harlan Miller

Candied Maple Walnuts

Melanie Lowe
Dover, DE

Real maple syrup makes these sweet & spicy nuts irresistible
for snacking...they're a super hostess gift too.

1/4 c. maple syrup	1 t. salt
2 c. walnut halves	1/2 t. pepper
2 T. dark brown sugar, packed	1/4 to 1/2 t. cinnamon

Drizzle syrup over walnuts and toss to coat well. Mix remaining ingredients in a small bowl; stir into nuts and set aside. Generously spray a 15"x10" jelly-roll pan with non-stick vegetable spray. Spread nuts on pan in a single layer. Bake, uncovered, at 325 degrees for 5 minutes; turn nuts over. Reduce oven to 300 degrees. Bake an additional 5 to 8 minutes, until bubbly and deep golden, stirring twice and watching carefully to avoid burning. Remove pan to a wire rack. Break up any clumps; turn nuts onto wax paper. Store in an airtight container after completely cooled. Makes 2 cups.

Set a basket with Christmas crackers by the door...
a take-home treat for guests. Roll short lengths of
cardboard tube in giftwrap and fasten with a bit of tape.
Slip a plastic-wrapped treat inside each tube. Twist the
ends of the giftwrap and tie with narrow ribbon...clever!

Cranberry Christmas Punch

Francie Stutzman
Dalton, OH

A warm and welcoming beverage to greet your friends
as they come into your home at Christmastime.

3-oz. pkg. cherry gelatin mix
1 c. boiling water
6-oz. can frozen lemonade
   or pineapple-lemonade
   concentrate

3 c. cold water
32-oz. bottle cranberry juice
   cocktail
32-oz. bottle ginger ale, chilled

Dissolve gelatin mix in boiling water; stir in frozen concentrate. Pour into a large pitcher along with cold water and cranberry juice; chill. At serving time, slowly add ginger ale. Serves 6 to 8.

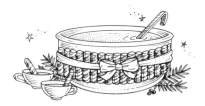

So-Simple Eggnog

Denise Mainville
Huber Heights, OH

When we were kids, we were allowed to drink this eggnog from the
"special" glasses...that was always such a big deal to us!

1/2 gal. milk, divided
3.4-oz. pkg. instant vanilla
   pudding mix
1/4 c. sugar

2 t. vanilla extract
1/2 t. cinnamon
1/2 t. nutmeg

In a large bowl or pitcher, whisk 3/4 cup milk and pudding mix until smooth. Whisk in sugar, vanilla and spices until sugar dissolves; stir in remaining milk. Chill before serving. Makes 16 servings.

Spinach-Stuffing Balls

Sue Berte
Chester, NY

This is a recipe I have used for years as an appetizer. They always disappear quickly...even my kids who don't like spinach go crazy for them!

10-oz. pkg. frozen chopped
    spinach, cooked and drained
6-oz. pkg. chicken-flavored
    stuffing mix

1 egg, beaten
1/2 c. grated Parmesan cheese

Stir all ingredients together in a large bowl. Form mixture into balls by teaspoonfuls. Place on a buttered baking sheet. Bake at 350 degrees for 10 to 12 minutes, to desired crunchiness. Serve hot. Makes 12 servings.

After-Christmas sales are a great time to stock up!
Look for solid-colored giftwrap, ribbon, candles and
even twinkle lights...perfect for year 'round
decorating, crafting and entertaining.

Sweet Italian Beef

Sarah Ricklic
New Philadelphia, OH

A warm and cozy "home sweet home" dish that holds a special place in my heart! We prepared it the week before my wedding, when we had lots of family & friends helping with the final details. Quick, delicious and easy to make in a slow cooker.

2 to 3-lb. beef chuck roast
16-oz. bottle Italian salad
   dressing
1/4 c. brown sugar, packed

2 T. Italian seasoning,
   or to taste
8 to 10 sandwich buns, split

Place roast in a slow cooker. Drizzle salad dressing over roast; sprinkle with brown sugar. Cover and cook on low setting for 10 to 12 hours. When roast is tender, remove it from slow cooker and shred with 2 forks. Stir seasoning into sauce in slow cooker. Return shredded roast to slow cooker and stir to combine. Spoon onto sandwich buns or serve as open-faced sandwiches. Serves 8 to 10.

Offer a variety of mini buns for party sandwiches so guests can enjoy sampling several different fillings. They're easier to handle too! Brown & serve rolls work well...you're sure to find others in the bakery department of your local grocery.

Creamy Cherry Dip

Pamela Rodriguez
Newalla, OK

My mother used to make this filling to bake in a graham cracker pie crust, and I adapted it to serve as a yummy sweet dip. It's a Thanksgiving and Christmas tradition at our house.

3-oz. pkg. cream cheese,
  softened
2-2/3 c. powdered sugar
16-oz. container frozen
  whipped topping, thawed

21-oz. can cherry pie filling
graham crackers

Place cream cheese in a large bowl; add powdered sugar and mix well. Fold in whipped topping and pie filling. Serve with graham crackers for dipping. Makes 8 to 10 servings.

Start a simple holiday scrapbook to update every year with the family's Christmas card, giftwrap samples, copies of letters to Santa, notes from special guests and of course holiday snapshots...such fun to look at year after year!

Black Forest Fondue

Arlene Smulski
Lyons, IL

This chocolatey fondue was selected for a get-together I was having with some friends. I was considering a retro theme, something classic but a little unusual that would go well with coffee & tea. It was a very big success!

3/4 c. whipping cream
1/8 t. salt
1 c. milk chocolate chips
1 c. semi-sweet chocolate chips

2-1/2 T. cherry extract
1 T. corn syrup
pound cake cubes, assorted
   fruit cubes and slices

In a saucepan over medium heat, bring cream and salt to a boil. Remove from heat. Add chocolates to saucepan; cover and let stand for a few minutes. Uncover; whisk until smooth. Whisk in extract and corn syrup. Serve immediately with pound cake and fruit. May be kept warm in a slow cooker or fondue pot over low heat; stir often. Makes 10 servings.

Take the kids to a paint-your-own pottery shop. They'll love decorating a plate and mug especially for Santa's milk & cookies...you'll love making memories together.

Special Pork Barbecue

Kimberly Nicewander
Hollidaysburg, PA

My great-aunt used to prepare this wonderful barbecue at
a restaurant she owned in the 1950s. My husband enjoys
topping his sandwich with coleslaw...yummy!

2 to 3-lb. pork roast	1 T. lemon juice
2 t. oil, divided	2 T. brown sugar, packed
2 to 3 c. water	1 t. salt
1 c. onion, diced	1 T. Worcestershire sauce
1 c. celery, diced	1 c. catsup
2 T. vinegar	6 hearty rolls, split

In a Dutch oven over medium-high heat, brown pork in one
teaspoon oil. Add enough water to cover roast. Reduce heat to
medium-low. Simmer until roast is tender and falls apart easily,
about 2 to 3 hours. Or, place roast in a slow cooker with 2 cups of
water; cover and cook on low setting for 8 to 10 hours, until tender.
Drain, reserving one cup cooking liquid. Shred roast with 2 forks
and set aside. In a large saucepan, sauté onion and celery in
remaining oil. Add reserved cooking liquid and remaining ingredients
except rolls. Cook over low heat until hot and bubbly. Add shredded
pork to saucepan and heat through. Serve on hearty rolls. Serves 6.

You do so much for everyone else during the holidays...
remember to treat yourself! Savor a mug of hot cocoa
while reading a favorite Christmas story or just take a few
minutes to enjoy the sounds and scents of the season.

Savory Sausage Balls

Lori Hoffman
Gibsonia, PA

These tasty treats are a must for the Christmas Eve festivities at our house. They're a great make-ahead appetizer too...assemble and fry them ahead of time, then freeze until you are ready to bake them.

8-oz. pkg. ground pork
   sausage
1/4 c. onion, finely chopped
14-1/2 oz. jar sauerkraut,
   drained and chopped
1 c. plus 2 T. dry bread crumbs,
   divided
3-oz. pkg. cream cheese,
   softened

1 t. mustard
2 T. dried parsley
1/8 t. garlic salt
1/4 t. pepper
2 eggs, beaten
1/4 c. milk
1/4 c. all-purpose flour
oil for frying

Brown sausage in a skillet over medium heat; drain. Add onion, sauerkraut and 2 tablespoons bread crumbs to skillet; mix well and set aside. Blend cream cheese, mustard and seasonings in a small bowl. Add to skillet and stir until well blended. Transfer mixture into a large bowl; refrigerate for one hour. Whisk eggs and milk together in a bowl. Mix flour and remaining bread crumbs in a shallow plate. Roll sausage mixture into one-inch balls. Dip in egg mixture and then roll in crumb mixture. Heat oil in a skillet over medium-high heat; fry balls in oil until golden on all sides. Drain; place in an ungreased 9"x9" baking pan. Bake, uncovered, at 375 degrees for 20 minutes. Makes about 2 dozen.

make a joyful noise!

When serving appetizers, a good rule of thumb for quantities is 6 to 8 per person if dinner will follow...12 to 15 per person if it's an appetizer-only gathering. Enjoy!

Cheesy Broccoli Dip

Diana Chaney
Olathe, KS

For a pretty presentation, edge the plate of warm dip with extra chopped broccoli to look like a Christmas wreath. Add a bow made of pimento strips...so clever!

1 c. mayonnaise-style salad
  dressing
10-oz. pkg. frozen chopped
  broccoli, thawed and
  drained
2-oz. jar diced pimentos,
  drained

1/2 c. grated Parmesan cheese
1 c. shredded mozzarella
  cheese, divided
wheat snack crackers

Combine salad dressing, broccoli, pimentos, Parmesan cheese and 1/2 cup mozzarella cheese. Spread in an ungreased 9" pie plate. Bake, uncovered, at 350 degrees for 20 to 25 minutes. Top with remaining mozzarella. Return to oven for 5 minutes, or until cheese is melted. Serve warm with crackers. Makes 3 cups.

A bowl of brightly colored surprise balls doubles as both party favors and an unusual centerpiece. Wind strips of crêpe paper into balls, tucking in tiny trinkets, charms, toys and fortunes between twists of the paper. Heap the balls in a punch bowl...what fun as the paper is unwound to reveal the treasures!

Easy Salmon Spread

Julie Garrett
Stafford, NY

My family's favorite appetizer for the holidays...I'm happy to share it with you!

8-oz. container sour cream
8-oz. pkg. cream cheese, softened
.7-oz. env. Italian salad dressing mix

6-oz. can salmon, drained and flaked
assorted crackers

Combine all ingredients except crackers; mix well and chill. Serve with crackers. Makes about 2 cups.

Make a party tray of savory appetizer tarts...guests will never suspect how easy it is! Bake frozen mini phyllo shells according to package directions, then spoon in a favorite creamy dip or spread.

Baked Jalapeño Poppers

Ann Aucelli
Painesville, OH

We host a biweekly Bible study in our home and serve a variety of snacks to go with the study. Here's a spicy favorite!

8-oz. pkg. cream cheese,
  softened
1 c. shredded Cheddar cheese
1 c. shredded Monterey Jack
  cheese
6 slices bacon, crisply cooked
  and crumbled
1/4 t. chili powder

1/4 t. garlic powder
1/4 t. salt
1 lb. jalapeño peppers, halved
  lengthwise and seeded
1/2 c. dry bread crumbs
Garnish: sour cream, onion dip,
  ranch salad dressing

Combine cheeses, bacon and seasonings; mix well. Spoon about 2 tablespoons of cheese mixture into each pepper half. Roll in bread crumbs to coat. Place on a greased baking sheet. Bake, uncovered, at 300 degrees: 20 minutes for spicy flavor; 30 minutes for medium flavor; 40 minutes for mild flavor. Serve warm with desired garnish. Makes 8 to 10 servings.

A speedy gift for a crafty friend! Fill a Mason jar with vintage buttons, mini thread spools and other sewing notions. Top the lid with batting and a circle of homespun, add a few pearl-headed pins and it's ready to give. She'll love it!

Slow-Cooker Corn Chowder

Gloria Robertson
Midland, TX

The perfect chowder for a cold, wintry day. It's so versatile,
it's even delicious spooned over corn chips.

32-oz. pkg. frozen shredded
  hashbrowns, thawed and
  patted dry
2 c. cooked ham or chicken,
  cubed
15-1/4 oz. can corn
14-3/4 oz. can creamed corn
10-3/4 oz. can cream of
  mushroom soup

10-3/4 oz. can cream of
  chicken soup
2-1/2 c. milk
1 onion, chopped
2 T. butter
2 T. dried parsley
salt and pepper to taste

In a slow cooker, combine all ingredients; mix well. Cover and cook
on low setting for 6 hours. Makes 8 servings.

Fill up the slow cooker with a hearty dinner in the
morning. After supper, you'll be able to get an early
start on a cozy family evening together, watching a
favorite holiday movie like *A Christmas Story*
or *Miracle on 34th Street.*

Marinated Shrimp Appetizer

Gail Konschak
Millville, NJ

*If you're looking for a really special appetizer for your holiday
party, this is it! It's delicious but really simple to prepare.
I'm asked for this recipe every time I serve it.*

2 onions, thinly sliced
1-1/2 c. oil
1-1/2 c. white vinegar
1/2 c. sugar
1/4 c. capers with juice

1-1/2 t. celery seed
1-1/2 t. salt
2 lbs. medium shrimp,
    cooked and peeled

Combine all ingredients except shrimp in a large bowl; mix well.
Add shrimp. Cover and refrigerate for 6 hours or longer, stirring
every hour or so. Drain shrimp, discarding marinade. Arrange
shrimp on a serving platter. Serves 8 to 10.

A no-cook appetizer that's ready in moments!
Unwrap a log of herbed goat cheese and roll it in
chopped fresh parsley. Place it on a serving dish and
surround with crisp crackers.

Garlic Pizza Wedges

Lisa LaGaipa
Monroe, CT

These flavorful wedges are so addictive! They're ready to serve in a jiffy too. A tasty change when you want something different from the same ol' snack foods.

1 Italian pizza crust
1 c. mayonnaise
1 c. grated Parmesan cheese
1 shallot, chopped
3-1/2 t. garlic, minced
1 T. dried oregano

Place pizza crust on a 14" pizza stone or ungreased pizza pan. Combine remaining ingredients; spread over pizza crust. Bake at 450 degrees for 8 to 10 minutes, or until edges of crust are lightly golden. Cut into thin wedges. Serves 8 to 12.

Adopt a special food tradition to enjoy each year as your family trims the tree. Whether it's a buffet of finger foods and spiced cider, sugar cookies and hot cocoa or something else of your own choosing, you'll be making heartfelt memories together.

Ham & Swiss Envelopes

Jackie Smulski
Lyons, IL

These yummy bites look complicated but are easy to make using refrigerated crescent-roll dough. They're a great addition to a Christmas card party.

3/4 c. cooked ham, diced
1 T. onion, finely chopped
1 t. oil
3/4 c. shredded Swiss cheese
3-oz. pkg. cream cheese, softened and cubed

2 8-oz. tubes refrigerated crescent rolls
1 T. fresh parsley, minced

In a skillet over medium heat, sauté ham and onion in oil until tender. Add cheeses and cook for several minutes, until melted. Remove from heat and set aside. Unroll crescent dough and separate each tube into 4 rectangles; press to seal perforations. Place 2 tablespoons of cheese mixture in the center of each rectangle. Top with parsley. Starting on one short side, fold 1/3 of the dough over filling. On the other short side, bring both corners together in the center to form a point. Fold over to resemble an envelope and pinch seams to seal. Arrange on an ungreased baking sheet. Bake at 375 degrees for 10 minutes. Serve immediately. Makes 8 servings.

Dress up some plain tea towels for the holidays...stitch bright red or green ribbon trim to the edges.

Twenty-Four Days 'Til Christmas Box

scrapbooking, giftwrap or
other decorative paper
scissors
upright rectangular tin
box with lid
craft glue
6 to 8 3-inch ribbons in a
variety of colors

colored markers
24 pieces of cardstock, cut
to fit inside box
Optional: stickers, other
craft supplies

Cut paper to size to cover outside of tin box base and top of lid. Glue in place. Glue ribbons to the top of the lid in a cluster to create a whimsical bow. Use markers to write a different idea for a fun activity on each piece of cardstock, decorating as desired. Place the cards in the box, replace the lid and give to your favorite child on December 1st.

Handmade from the Heart

Cozy Patchwork Scarf

20 4-inch sqs. felted wool in a variety of colors
1/4 yd. coordinating cotton fabric for lining

embroidery needle and embroidery thread
sewing machine or needle and sewing thread

Lay out the felted squares, 2 to a row. With wrong sides together, blanket-stitch squares together in pairs using an embroidery needle and thread. Open pairs flat; blanket-stitch together to create one long scarf. Cut cotton lining fabric to same size. Pin scarf and lining together, right sides together. Machine or hand-stitch together with a 1/4-inch seam allowance, leaving an 8-inch long opening. Turn scarf right-side out through opening; slip-stitch closed. Blanket-stitch around edge of scarf. Machine or hand-stitch a 4-inch horizontal buttonhole across the center of second row of patches. Carefully cut buttonhole open. For a snug, cozy fit that's like a warm hug, thread the end of the scarf through the buttonhole.

Felted Wool:

washing machine
100% wool fabric
zippered laundry bag
liquid laundry detergent
clothes dryer

Set up washing machine for heavy-duty cycle with hot-water wash. Place wool fabric in a zippered laundry bag. Add detergent (1/3 capful for small load; 1/2 capful for medium; 3/4 capful for large). Wash fabric for full machine cycle. Machine-dry on high heat in clothes dryer. Cut felted wool to desired size.

Lavender-Mint Eye Pillow

8-inch sq. cotton fabric
sewing needle and thread
1/2 c. flax seed

1/3 c. dried lavender
2 T. dried peppermint
3 drops lavender essential oil

Fold fabric in half, wrong sides together. Stitch together on long side and one short side, leaving the other short side open. Turn pillow right-side out. In a small bowl, combine flax seed, lavender buds, peppermint leaves and lavender oil; mix well. Spoon mixture into the pillow; turn in raw edges and stitch closed.

I'm dreaming of a white Christmas,
Just like the ones I used to know.
—Irving Berlin

Frosty Etched Glass Jar

glass jar with lid
rubbing alcohol
cotton balls
Optional: painter's tape

vinyl stick-on letters
etching cream
paintbrush
acrylic paint

With these basic instructions, you can decorate jars for gift mixes or personalize jar candles...almost anything that's made of glass! Wash and dry your hands thoroughly before decorating glass surfaces, as oils can leave fingerprints. Peel or soak off jar label. Remove any sticky residue with rubbing alcohol and cotton balls; wash jar and allow to dry. If you want only a certain area to have a frosted look, use painter's tape to mark off the area to be etched. Attach letters to spell out your message; press firmly. Cover work surface well with old newspapers. Brush a thick layer of etching cream onto glass. Let stand for the amount of time indicated by manufacturer's instructions. Rinse off cream in warm water, in a stainless-steel sink only, not porcelain. Pat dry; peel off letters and tape. To finish, paint jar lid with acrylic paint.

Santa's Fleecy Gift Bag

Wrap up oversized gifts with this easy-to-make gift bag.

3 yds. fleece print fabric
straight pins
sewing machine and thread

safety pin
12-ft. spool ribbon,
1-1/2 inch wide

Fold fabric in half with right sides together, matching selvages. Pin long edges together. On one long edge, 3 inches down from top edge, mark a 1-3/4 inch opening for a casing. Sew long edges with a 1/2-inch seam allowance, leaving marked area open. To form casing, fold top edges down 2-1/2 inches toward the inside of bag. Pin and stitch along edge of casing. Sew an edge stitch 1/4-inch from top of folded edge. Turn bag right-side out. Fasten a safety pin to one end of ribbon. Feed the pin and ribbon through the side opening and pull through casing. Tie ribbon in a bow; trim ends of ribbon.

Handmade from the Heart

Sweet Potpourri Balls

paintbrush
acrylic paint in a color to match
  potpourri mix
4-inch dia. plastic foam
  craft balls

hot-glue gun and glue sticks
1/2-inch wide ribbon
straight pins
craft glue
dried potpourri mix

Paint foam balls and let dry. Hot-glue one or 2 lengths of ribbon around each ball as desired; pin in place and let dry. Remove pins. Spread craft glue over uncovered areas on ball; sprinkle generously with potpourri mix. Use hot glue to attach any larger pieces of potpourri and, if desired, a ribbon bow at the top.

Bottle-Cap Magnets

craft knife or 1-inch circular
  craft punch
holiday cards
craft glue

soft drink bottle caps
clear casting resin
button magnets
silicone cement

Use a craft knife or circular punch to cut out small designs from holiday cards in one-inch circles. Glue each design to the inside of a bottle cap; let dry. Fill bottle caps to the rim with casting resin, following manufacturer's instructions; let dry overnight. Attach magnets to back of bottle caps with silicone cement; let dry overnight.

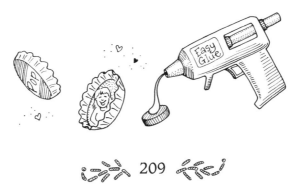

Gadget Barn

sturdy shoebox with lid
decorative paper
craft glue
pencil and eraser
craft knife

Optional: 1/2-inch metal
  eyelets or grommets,
  eyelet tool and hammer
electric power strip

Keep all the cords of cellphones and other electronic gadgets neat
and tidy in this handy desktop box! Cover box as desired with
decorative paper and craft glue. Cover lid separately and set aside.
Use a pencil to lightly measure and mark 4 to 5, 1/2-inch circles
along the front side of box. Lightly measure and mark a one-inch
circle on the back of the box for the power strip's plug. Cut out holes
with craft knife; erase pencil marks. If desired, insert eyelets or
grommets in holes in front of box and set them, using tool and
hammer. Place power strip inside box; pull its cord through the hole
in the back and replace the lid.

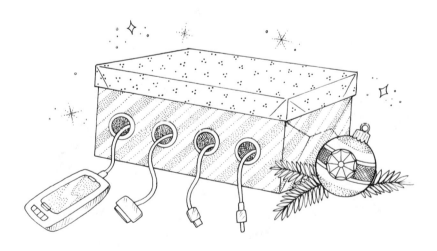

Charming Yo-Yo Garland

6-inch saucer
scrap of cardboard
pencil
scissors
1/2-yd. cotton print fabric in
   coordinating colors

Optional: steam iron
sewing needle
strong thread or embroidery
   floss
1 to 2 yds. 1/4-inch ribbon
hot glue gun and glue sticks

To make a yo-yo template, trace around a saucer onto cardboard and cut out the circle. On the wrong side of fabric, trace around the template with a pencil. Cut out as many circles as desired. For each yo-yo, fold under 1/4 inch all around the edge of the circle; press with an iron, if desired. Using a needle and strong thread or embroidery floss, stitch a running stitch all around the circle, staying close to the folded edge. Leave a few inches of thread at the end. Gently pull the thread until the edges meet in the center. Take your time and shape the gathers as you go. Knot and trim your thread. Use your hands to flatten the yo-yo. Hot-glue the finished yo-yos onto the ribbon to create a garland. There are so many clever ways to use these whimsical little circles of fabric...decorate gift tags, Christmas stockings or a jar of homemade jam. You're sure to think of others!

Stained-Glass Votives

baby food or other small jars
rubbing alcohol
cotton balls
tissue paper in assorted colors
scissors
liquid starch

spray bottle
Optional: découpage medium,
  paintbrush
1/4-inch wide ribbon
tealight candles

Peel or soak off jar labels; discard lids. Remove any sticky residue
with rubbing alcohol and cotton balls; wash jars and allow to dry.
Cut or tear tissue paper into 1/2-inch squares. Pour liquid starch into
spray bottle. Spray starch on outside of jar. Randomly apply paper
squares over surface of jar until completely covered; let dry. If
desired, add a coat of découpage medium. Tie a ribbon around neck
of jars and place tealights inside.

Handmade from the Heart

Festive Flowerpot

terra-cotta pot with saucer
paintbrushes
acrylic paints
pencil

Optional: tracing paper,
transfer paper
water-based varnish

If using an old flowerpot, scrub it well with soap and water; let dry overnight. New pots are ready to paint. Use a paintbrush to apply 2 basecoats of paint to saucer and outside of pot; let dry after each coat. Lightly draw a design on the pot. Trace template (below) or other design onto tracing paper. Tape the tracing onto the pot, slip transfer paper underneath and trace over the design lines with a pencil. To repeat design, reposition tracing and transfer papers as needed. Paint the design as desired; let dry. Erase any pencil marks. Apply water-based varnish to saucer and outside of pot, following manufacturer's instructions. Let dry before adding a poinsettia or Christmas cactus. A thoughtful hostess gift!

Spicy Scented Kitchen Trivet

2 9-inch sqs. sturdy cotton
   fabric
straight pins
sewing machine or needle
   and thread

2 T. whole cloves
4 4-inch cinnamon sticks,
   broken in half
2 to 3 c. long-cooking rice,
   uncooked

Pin fabric squares together, right sides together. Stitch around the edges with a 1/4-inch seam allowance; leave a 1-1/2 inch opening. Trim corners and turn right-side out. Add spices and enough rice to fill fairly full. Slip-stitch the opening closed.

Snowflake Window Clings

tracing paper
pencil
baking sheet

wax paper
dimensional white or icy blue
   glitter fabric paint

Trace a snowflake design (below) onto tracing paper and enlarge on a copier, or draw one of your own. Lay pattern face-up on a baking sheet and cover it with a piece of wax paper. Using fabric paint and 1/8-inch wide lines, trace over the pattern lines on the wax paper; make sure all lines connect. Repeat as desired; let dry overnight. Carefully peel snowflakes from wax paper and apply to windows.

Handmade from the Heart

Sparkly Snow Scene

3 assorted-size glass jars
   with lids
1 yd. 1-inch ribbon
scissors
hot-glue gun

2 to 4 c. sea salt or Epsom salt
small pine branches and
   pine cones
small ornaments or figures

Remove jar lids and set aside. Measure and cut a length of ribbon
to fit around each jar, one inch below rims. Hot-glue ribbon in place.
Fill each jar 1/4 full of salt. Arrange branches, pine cones and small
ornaments inside jars; don't overcrowd. Replace jar lids. Arrange the
jars in the center of the table or on a cake stand. Arrange more
branches around jars, if desired.

Handy Totes, Two Ways

Appliqué Tote:

canvas tote bag
wax paper
4 to 6 5-inch sqs. cotton fabric
pinking shears

fabric glue
sewing needle and thread
buttons, beads, charms, other
    embellishments

Lay tote bag out flat; tuck sheets of wax paper inside tote bag to prevent glue from soaking through. Use pinking shears to cut a decorative edge around each fabric square. Arrange squares on tote as desired; attach with fabric glue. Let dry; discard wax paper. Use needle and thread to attach embellishments as desired.

Photo Transfer Tote:

digital photo
computer and inkjet printer
iron-on transfer paper

scissors
steam iron and ironing board
canvas tote bag

Upload or scan selected photo to a computer. Print photo onto a sheet of iron-on transfer paper. Cut out image with scissors. Iron image onto tote bag according to manufacturer's instructions.

Cedar Sneaker Stuffers

1/4 yd. cotton fabric
scissors
sewing machine or needle
and thread

cedar shavings from a pet store
Optional: 12 inches decorative
cording

Cut 2 pieces from fabric, each measuring 17 inches by 3 inches. Fold each piece in half lengthwise, matching short ends, with wrong sides together. Sew the 2 long sides together with a 1/4-inch seam allowance, leaving one end open. Turn fabric right-side out to form a tube. Divide cedar shavings between the 2 tubes, stuffing loosely, and sew closed. If desired, insert one end of the cording into each short end as it's being sewn closed; secure with several stitches.

Cute-as-a-Button Framed Photo

paintbrush
wood sealer
7-inch by 5-inch unfinished
    wood plaque
acrylic paint

6-inch by 4-inch photo
craft glue
assorted buttons of similar
    color

Frame the children's photo as a gift for Grandma & Grandpa, or make a pretty tabletop decoration...use a favorite Christmas card instead of a photo. Brush a coat of wood sealer onto plaque; let dry. Clean paintbrush and apply 2 to 3 coats of acrylic paint; let dry after each coat. Use craft glue sparingly to attach photo to the surface of the plaque; let dry. To decorate the edges, arrange and glue on buttons so they overlap where edges of photo meet the plaque. Let dry.

Stitch-in-Time Mini Sewing Kit

small tin box from mints
  or candy
spray paint for metal
scrap of scrapbooking paper
scissors
craft glue

2-inch length magnetic
  strip tape
sewing needles, straight pins,
  tiny scissors and other
  sewing items

For a gift that's oh-SEW-special...transform a pocket-size tin into a
handy sewing kit! Open the tin and lay it flat on a newspaper-
covered surface, open-side down. Apply spray paint to the outside
of tin. Measure and cut scrapbook paper to cover the lid. Glue paper
onto the lid; let dry. Attach the magnetic strip tape to the inside of
the lid. Place needles and pins on magnetic strip. Arrange other
sewing kit items inside tin.

INDEX

Appetizers

Baked Jalapeño Poppers, 198
Black Forest Fondue, 193
Cheesy Broccoli Dip, 196
Chinese Chicken Spread, 183
Creamy Cherry Dip, 192
Easy Salmon Spread, 197
Festive Cranberry Salsa, 182
Garlic Pizza Wedges, 201
Glazed Chicken Wings, 185
Ham & Swiss Envelopes, 202
Marinated Shrimp Appetizer, 200
Mississippi Fun Dip, 184
Patricia's Super Nachos, 187
Savory Sausage Balls, 195
Spinach-Stuffing Balls, 190
Vintage Party Mix, 186

Beverages

Christmas Brew, 37
Cranberry Christmas Punch, 189
Holiday Wassail, 37
Let-It-Snow Cocoa, 55
So-Simple Eggnog, 189

Breads

Best-Ever Italian Bread, 98
Cheesy Garlic Pull-Apart Bread, 53
Connie's Pretzel Buns, 49
Fresh Jalapeño Cornbread, 51
Golden Drop Biscuits, 38
Ham & Cheddar Cornbread, 65
Holiday Eggnog Bread, 55
Homemade Crescent Rolls, 105
Mini Butterscotch Drop Scones, 54
Mrs. Claus' Christmas Bread, 23
Zesty Orange Mini Muffins, 31

Breakfast

Amish Hashbrowns, 33
Baked Brown Sugar Oatmeal, 27
Baked Spiced French Toast, 34
Captain Harris's Seafood Quiche, 104
Cherry Streusel Coffee Cake, 22
Christmas Morn Sausage Bake, 24
Cranberry Christmas Canes, 42
Crispy Maple Bacon, 28
Crustless Broccoli Quiche, 40
Ham & Cheese Quiche, 32
Mini Cheddar Soufflés, 39
Nan's Cinnamon Rolls, 35
Pistachio Coffee Cake, 36
Sausage Breakfast Pie, 41
Spinach & Mozzarella Quiche, 25
Umm's Breakfast Casserole, 29
Winter Fried Apples, 26

Candies

Candied Maple Walnuts, 188
Cherry-Walnut Fudge, 167
Chocolate-Oat Fudge, 176
Coconut-Almond Candies, 168
Cream Cheese Fudge, 171
Holiday Hard Candy, 178
Holiday Strawberries, 166
Homemade Caramels, 175
Microwave Pecan Brittle, 169
Nutty Mixed-Up Popcorn, 170
Peanut Butter Crunch Candy, 177
Peanutty Chocolate Clusters, 173
Reindeer Chow, 172
Snowy Trail Mix, 179
Sunflower Seed Brittle, 180
Tasty Toffee Candy, 174

Cookies

Almond Butter Cookies, 164
Annabel's Pumpkin Cookies, 160
Brownie Thins, 146
Butter Pecan Cookies, 150
"Buttermilk" Cinnamon Bars, 149
Chocolate Oat Chews, 145
Chocolate Spice Cookies, 142
Christmas Meringues, 159
Cranberry Oat Cookies, 153
Grandma's Gingerbread Men, 163
Holly Jolly Cookies, 151
Jan Hagels, 155
Lemon-Macadamia Cookies, 148
Maple Pecan Drops, 143
Melt-in-Your-Mouth Cookies, 157
Mom's Waffle Cookies, 154
Orange Drop Cookies, 162

INDEX

Peppermint Bark Brownies, 139
Piña Colada Cookies, 158
Santa's Whiskers, 144
So-Yummy Chocolate Bars, 161
Soft Chocolate Chip Cookies, 152
Spicy Pepper Nuts, 147
Walnut Rugalach, 156

Desserts

Caramel-Glazed Apple Cake, 136
Cheery Cran-Pear Cobbler, 135
Cherry Brownie Cobbler, 130
Cider Apple Pie, 126
Cream Cheese Pumpkin Squares, 133
Creamy Eggnog Pie, 137
Fudgy Pudding Cake, 138
Honey Bun Cake, 132
Mini Pecan Tartlets, 127
Mocha Pudding Cake, 134
Molasses Chiffon Pie, 140
Pumpkin Ice Cream Pie, 128
Red Velvet Christmas Cake, 129
Sweet Cinnamon Pie, 131
Tapioca Fruit Delight, 30

Little Extras

Apple Pancake Syrup, 26
Chocolate Buttercream Frosting, 154
Country Sausage Gravy, 38
Crispy Butter Croutons, 59
Favorite Cookie Frosting, 157

Mains

Brown Sugar-Glazed Ham, 102
Cheesy Eggplant Casserole, 124
Dawn's Homemade Meatloaf, 68
Easy "Rotisserie" Chicken, 110
Feliz Navidad Casserole, 96
Gramp's Goulash, 74
Holiday Pork Loin, 92
Judy's Kickin' Chicken, 72
Last-Minute Lasagna, 89
Louisiana Chicken, 79
Morgan's Crabby Mac & Cheese, 80
Nut-Crusted Baked Chicken, 123
Oh-So-Easy Pot Roast Dinner, 70

Orange Chops & Rice Tango, 85
Quick & Easy Baked Fish, 81
Raspberry-Glazed Salmon, 115
Savory Roast Turkey Breast, 94
Simply Elegant Steak & Rice, 120
Special Baked Chicken, 69
Special Baked Lasagna, 99
Stuffed Bread, 58
Sweet-and-Sour Brisket, 106
Taco Skillet Dinner, 88

Salads

Becky's Artichoke-Rice Salad, 84
Black Cherry Cranberry Salad, 101
Crisp Celery-Pear Salad, 76
Spicy Cabbage-Apple Slaw, 87
Spicy Citrus Salad, 112
Tossed Salad & Cider Dressing, 113

Sandwiches

Beef Stroganoff Sandwich, 46
Beefy Taco Pockets, 50
Hot Turkey Sandwiches, 62
James Family Toasty Sub, 56
Pesto Chicken Paninis, 45
Special Pork Barbecue, 194
Sweet Italian Beef, 191

Sides

Almond Rice Pilaf, 114
Barley & Sweet Corn Bake, 118
Big Butterflies & Mushrooms, 77
Buttery Herbed Noodles, 71
Carrots Vichy, 82
Creamed Sweet Peas, 69
Favorite Sausage-Apple Stuffing, 116
Grandma's Swiss String Beans, 93
Holiday Broccoli Casserole, 121
Honey Sweet Potatoes, 108
Lemon-Chive Potatoes, 122
Maple-Baked Acorn Squash, 109
Mashed Potato Casserole, 78
Mexican Black-Eyed Peas, 97
Mom's Green Beans & Bacon, 75
Mom's Oyster Dressing, 119
Old-Time Pickled Peaches, 83

INDEX

Roasted Garlic Mashed Potatoes, 95
Sesame Asparagus, 81
Slow-Cooked Applesauce, 100
Speedy Chinese Noodles, 90
Speedy Skillet Pecan Rice, 73
Spiced Apple-Cranberry Sauce, 111
Susan's Famous Carrots, 107
Sweet Potato Soufflé, 117
Twice-Baked Potato Casserole, 103
Yam-a-Dandy, 83

Soups & Stews

Chill-Chaser Chicken Soup, 52
Creamy Tomato Tortellini Soup, 44
Curried Pumpkin Bisque, 48
Harvest Ham Chowder, 57
Herbed Chicken-Barley Soup, 47
Homemade Chicken-Tomato Stew, 63
Meatball Potato Soup, 60
Slow-Cooked Hearty Pork Stew, 66
Slow-Cooker 16-Bean Stew, 86
Slow-Cooker Corn Chowder, 199
Turkey & Wild Rice Soup, 61
Vegetarian Chili, 64

Crafty Gifts

Bottle-Cap Magnets, 209
Cedar Sneaker Stuffers, 217
Charming Yo-Yo Garland, 211
Cozy Patchwork Scarf, 205
Cute-as-a-Button Framed Photo, 218
Festive Flowerpot, 213
Frosty Etched Glass Jar, 207
Gadget Barn, 210
Handy Totes, Two Ways, 216
Lavender-Mint Eye Pillow, 206
Santa's Fleecy Gift Bag, 208
Snowflake Window Clings, 214
Sparkly Snow Scene, 215
Spicy Scented Kitchen Trivet, 214
Stained-Glass Votives, 212
Stitch-in-Time Mini Sewing Kit, 219
Sweet Potpourri Balls, 209
Twenty-Four Days 'Til Christmas
    Box, 204

Find Gooseberry Patch
wherever you are!

www.gooseberrypatch.com

Call us toll-free at 1·800·854·6673

handknit mittens • strings of popcorn • sugar cookies • homemade candy • holly & mistletoe • letters to Santa • curling ribbons • paper snowflakes

U.S. to Metric Recipe Equivalents

Volume Measurements

1/4 teaspoon	1 mL
1/2 teaspoon	2 mL
1 teaspoon	5 mL
1 tablespoon = 3 teaspoons	15 mL
2 tablespoons = 1 fluid ounce	30 mL
1/4 cup	60 mL
1/3 cup	75 mL
1/2 cup = 4 fluid ounces	125 mL
1 cup = 8 fluid ounces	250 mL
2 cups = 1 pint =16 fluid ounces	500 mL
4 cups = 1 quart	1 L

Weights

1 ounce	30 g
4 ounces	120 g
8 ounces	225 g
16 ounces = 1 pound	450 g

Oven Temperatures

300° F	150° C
325° F	160° C
350° F	180° C
375° F	190° C
400° F	200° C
450° F	230° C

Baking Pan Sizes

Square

8x8x2 inches	2 L = 20x20x5 cm
9x9x2 inches	2.5 L = 23x23x5 cm

Rectangular

13x9x2 inches	3.5 L = 33x23x5 cm

Loaf

9x5x3 inches	2 L = 23x13x7 cm

Round

8x1-1/2 inches	1.2 L = 20x4 cm
9x1-1/2 inches	1.5 L = 23x4 cm